Beyond Metaphor

Dialogue from the Realm of Self Knowledge

Ba Luvmour

Copyright: Ba Luvmour 2011. All rights reserved.

ISBN: 1475284926

ISBN-13: 9781475284928

Acknowledgements:

Josette, Amber, and Albee—Masters of unflinching acceptance

Jill Kelly—Editor *Extraordinaire*

My Teachers

Dedication:

To Ruby and Naomi

Table of Contents

Introduction: What Is Knowledge? xi
Chapter One: On Self-Inquiry and Self-Observation 1
   Who Was I? 3
     The Method.. 5
     The Human Thought Process... 7
      Surrender... 11
      Musings from Consciousness and Beyond 11
Chapter 2: Who is the Self in Self-knowledge? 15
      Food 18
      Adolescence 19
      Right Speech 21
      Green.. 25
     Conscience—the Necessary Foundation for Inquiry......................26
     Religion and Conscience..28
      Every Emotion Counts 30
     Separation, Perfection, Alienation, Compensation 33
     Three Aspects of Self..37
      Symbiosis 40
      If I Were A Painting… 40
      I Am Poetry 42
      When Selfishness Ends..................................... 45

  Happiness 45
  Miracle 46
Chapter Three: On Relationship, Conscience, and
Self-knowledge 47
  The End of Rejection 52
  Savior? 57
  This is Us, Me, We, I, and You 62
Chapter Four: On Meaning 65
  You are a Philosopher 69
Chapter Five: The Creative Flow of Need 71
  Dynamics 75
  Compassion 76
  Prophecy 79
  Place 85
  Last Words 89
  On Genius and Self-Knowledge 94
  The Only Skill That Counts 97
Chapter Six: On Non-Ordinary Experiences 101
  Early Journeys 101
  Preparation and Reentry 111
  Persecution 113
  Maps 115
  Devotion 117
  The Silent Sound 118
  Surrender Your I's 119
  Molten Gold 119
  The Preserver 120
  Sacred Ground 120
  Experience 122

Eagle Talk	124
Chapter Seven: Ethics	131
Mechanical Ethics	132
Smarmy Shock-Jock with Homophobic Undertones	136
Ordinary Extraordinary Experiences	138
Indentured to Death	141
Renunciation	142
Self-Knowledge	145
Silence	147
The End of Pollution	148
Chapter Eight: Living Self-Knowledge	149
Chapter Nine: Love	161
Beyond	171

Introduction: What Is Knowledge?

Q: You claim that living self-knowledge yields joy and well-being. But I am not sure what you mean by knowledge. There are so many uses of the word.

Ba: Knowledge is used in the sense of its ancient derivation from which we also have the words "kin" and "ken." It refers to an intimacy, a familiarity that is natural, respectful, and responsive. The word "ledge" originally referred to wedlock. That implies intimacy intensified. Knowledge is in our bones, beyond thinking or reasoning.

Q: I often think of two other meanings. One is data or information. Another is religious, like the Gnostics. You are saying something different.

Ba: I am. We have to let go of the commercial use of the word and its inference of acquiring, storing, retrieving; of using knowledge as currency to solve problems. And the religious notion is too esoteric. Self-knowledge is ours, embedded in and permeating our very selves. There is no need to confine it to religion or spirituality.

Q: Are you saying that knowledge is similar to understanding?

Ba: Yes and no. The Greek roots of the word actually specify understanding and "overstanding." And every other language uses at least two words to describe different facets of knowledge. As I said, I mean knowing that is beyond reason, beyond feeling, beyond street smarts and intuition. This knowledge may appear in these and many other forms, but the knowledge itself can only be known as self, as each of us, as you and as me.

Q: Okay, but why bother? What is the point of self-knowledge?

Ba: How can we not bother? In order to see the world, we first need to know who is looking. We must become intimate with ourselves.

Q: Wait a minute! I am me. I know what I see and think.

Ba: Tell me. Do you approve of murder or of environmental degradation?

Q: Of course not.

Ba: Lying?

Q: Horrible, and you can add greed and child molestation and…

Ba: Okay, I get it. But why do you care?

Q: Because I know there is a better way to live. I know that we can be free of these behaviors.

Ba: So you know that there is a greatness that lives in us? Something that pulls us towards well-being and all that implies?

Q: It seems that it must.

Ba: Have you actualized this greatness or this better way to live?

Q: No.

Ba: How do you know?

Q: Honestly, I don't know.

Ba: How do you know that you don't know?

Q: Two ways, one for sure and one a surmise. The for-sure way is that I certainly see greed and violence in myself. And, in truth, I don't just see it but have behaved that way at times. The surmise comes from philosophers, psychologists, educators, religionists, and others who speak of a greater wisdom.

Ba: Why believe them? Is learning *about* something the same as knowing it?

Q: No. Okay, so what you are saying is that I can uncover greater depths of this better life by knowing myself.

Ba: Well, it was you who said "I know what I think and see." So you were already referring to yourself as the source of knowledge. And now you are realizing that that there may be wider and deeper insights that can refine that seeing. And that accessing these deeper insights is a good thing to do.

Q: And you claim that I can find this in myself?

Ba: Yes. It's the only way that you can know it. Self is the only "place" where you can have confidence that this knowledge is true and real. No matter how many others talk about it, if you don't know it—if it's not in your bones—then you have only heard about it, which is certainly a secondhand experience.

Q: Okay, I'm almost ready to go on this journey. But there remains one significant obstacle. Who are you? What qualifies you to do this? And, equally important, why do you believe that anyone else can do what you have done?

Ba: Thank you. Great questions. To answer the last one first, I know that you cannot live the life I have lived. Indeed, I refuse to offer my life as an example. Trying to living another's life can only lead to unnecessary suffering.

At the same time our relationship is critical to each of us deepening self-knowledge. It requires mutual respect. Through our dialogue we co-emerge to find a new way of being together and with ourselves. Therefore, I must include my personal life. Abstract "teachings" are mostly ineffective.

Q: I appreciate that you insist that this journey cannot mean that anyone should live as you have. So how can you reconcile the need to avoid setting yourself up as an example and yet include yourself personally?

Ba: Two ways. First, I will bring relevant examples, anecdotes, and a few stories from my life and from the lives of others with whom I have been personally connected. Second, over the years I have written poems that speak of my direct experiences and tell some of the story of my life. I hope that these will be sufficient. And you have the responsibility to engage the personal revelations in the spirit in which they are intended. They intend relationship and connection, not morality or a path to follow. I intend transparency, but always in the service of elucidating self-knowledge.

Ready to rock?

Q: A bit nervous, but ready. From what we have talked about so far, I can sense that my familiar way of viewing myself and the world could be significantly altered. That is always somewhat frightening.

Ba: Frightening to whom?

Q: Let's go.

Chapter One:
On Self-Inquiry and Self-Observation

Ba: We begin with ourselves, as we are.

Q: As we must, I am sure. But if we are mired in partial, confused beliefs that prevent me from actualizing self-knowledge, then how can we have confidence in the self we find?

Ba: Self inquiry. Self inquiry will not make of you anything that you are not already; but it will, over time, destroy false beliefs. False beliefs are the root of suffering. Self-inquiry requires engaging inner struggle with ways we believe the world to be. In this way we overcome our ignorance and resistance and thereby come to self-knowledge. The purpose is to see into the nature of who we truly are. With reflection and self-inquiry, we are able live an authentic and integrated life.

Self-inquiry is the ability to inquire into our own thought processes and feelings and how we act on them and then react to them. Through the process of self-inquiry, we become aware of the many things we do automatically. This is can be an arduous process.

Q: Why arduous?

Ba: I asked the same question when I started. I thought: *Hey, I'll sit down, think about what I have done and try to understand it.* It might be that easy for some of us. And, in truth, it does become easier with practice. Once self-inquiry is second nature, I discovered that it is actually first nature. That it is our natural state—that this great gift is inherent in the human package.

Q: Then why is it arduous?

Ba: I will answer that later in some detail. And, if you like, I can offer the specific example of self-inquiry I have done with myself. But first, we need to talk about self-inquiry and self-observation. We have to know what they are and how they work before tackling why they are difficult to do for many of us.

Q: Fair enough.

Ba: The practice of self-inquiry leads to becoming conscious of formerly unconscious processes in ourselves. This is how shifts towards self-knowledge can begin to occur. It is an invaluable tool for gaining insight into life patterns, feelings, or underlying motivations. It requires time for quiet reflection yet, as a learned skill, it can take place in a moment. Eventually we realize that self-inquiry requires no special setting. However, in the beginning, it is helpful to create a quiet context to support undisturbed inner reflection. Through the method and practice of reflection and self-inquiry, inner wisdom, which is an equivalent term to self-knowledge, can become a reality. Inquiring into the nature of one's self that is in bondage, and realizing one's true nature, leads to release and transformation.

Q: Hold on. You just referred to inquiring into our bondage. I thought we were looking for a higher self, one that knows joy and love.

Ba: If we look for that, we will only find our projection of what we believe it to be. Visualize inner lights for a long time with great intensity and you will probably see them. The human imagination is that powerful. And your desire to find a certain self is a hint as to why the process is often arduous.

Our intention is to see who we are as we are. Self-knowledge does not need to be found. It is not an "it" or a "that."

Before we turn to the methodology, here's a poem about the event that pushed me over the edge and into self-inquiry.

Who Was I?

In my youth I married my woman-image,
Scripted my own myth,
And lived it with full conviction.

Chapter One: On Self-Inquiry and Self-Observation

One day the phone rang.
Sister dead of an overdose.
Two children bereft.
Image dissolved, myth busted.

I walked across America.
No electric body singing.
Just holed up in the Badlands.
Trying to breathe.

How could I be so dumb
To ignore death?
How could I think
That thinking led to freedom?

The Method

Ba: The process of self-inquiry is so simple that it can be explained in a few words. To practice you simply look directly into yourself in this present moment. Look into:
- What you sense, what you think, and what you feel
- The nature of the mind itself—thought, concepts, beliefs
- Look into your emotions—the pain, desires, joys, and what you wish could/should be
- The plain and undeniable "fact" of you in this moment

Then look beyond the thoughts, sensations, and feelings into the "who" or the "I" that is looking. What remains?

Q: That sounds like self-observation, not self-inquiry.

Ba: Yes, it is. Self-inquiry begins with self-observation. Self-observation is done in each moment. My experience with myself and others suggests it is too difficult at first to observe in each moment. It's easier to begin with reflection and inquiry. Then, as you begin to see the unconscious basis of most actions, you will either embrace the process of self-observation and self-inquiry or hide and deny.

Q: Does self-observation become easier?

Ba: Yes. The capacity for self-observation is natural. But the development of capacities depends upon relationship. If a child is not given a mother tongue by the time she is 4 or so, she will never speak a language. The capacity is innate but the development depends upon relationship. Language-rich environments lead to robust verbal-linguistic expression. Most of us did not have an education that provided the relationships that developed our self-observation capacity. That's another hint as to why the process is difficult for so many of us.

So we start with reflection and inquiry. When the mind becomes quiet, the motivation and meaning of action and relationship become clearer. We get to see the hidden aspects. We get to see that most of our life is governed by our thoughts. But we haven't looked at what these thoughts are based on, where they come from, or why we accept them.

Q: I was right to be frightened.

Ba: That I who is frightened is most likely held together by a web of unexamined thoughts.

Q: What do you mean?

Ba: You are asking: What is the nature of thought? Have you asked yourself that question?

Q: Not in a serious way. Just dabbling at the edges, so to speak, with readings in psychology, poetry, and philosophy. But no, I have never inquired deeply into my own thought processes. It feels slightly crazy and embarrassing to admit it.

Ba: Join the crowd. So we will look at thought in a minute. First, though it may be fleeting in the early stages of engaging reflection and inquiry there are moments when meaning "appears" and yields a larger perspective than one solely based on behavior, conditioning, or on the construction of social relationships. Most of us recognize and rejoice in this AH-HA moment but too few of us examine its origins through self-observation and self-inquiry.

Q: What happens when you do?

Ba: That is for each of us to find out. <u>Transformation must involve a substantial revision of assumptions and habits of mind with their resulting points of view</u>. These moments provide the field in new meaning can take place. Connecting to new meaning is the joy of self-discovery. Engaging self inquiry builds trust; self inquiry is the bridge to self-knowledge.

The Human Thought Process

Ba: Thought is time-bound. Thoughts based on the past simply carry the past into the future. Habits of mind often go unquestioned. When a thought goes unquestioned, the focus tends to be outward towards the outcomes of the thoughts instead of inward towards our own thinking processes. We look in the wrong direction.

Q: I need to try this on and see if it fits. I have the thought that I like talking with you. Typically I would say, "Okay, good, let's keep the conversation going." You are suggesting I turn to the source of the thought. Here goes. I can feel the care you feel for me, and for people and for life. That is warming and attractive. This dialogue also partially slakes my thirst for understanding myself and life. How's that?

Ba: Right direction, but it still only scratches the surface. The thirst and the warmth are useful self-observations. Self-observation attempts to see the moment without judgment. It...

Q: *Without judgment*?! That is impossible.

Ba: I agree that it starts that way. Judgment is ingrained in most thoughts. However, combined with self- inquiry, the source and value of the judgment are revealed. That revelation takes as long as it takes for each of us. Questions that expedite the insight into judgment and allow for self-observations ask: What is their source? How did they arise? Are there personal prejudicial predispositions? Are the judgments learned or embedded in human life?

Different questions may work for you. The question is always more important than the answer.

Q: It's a bit hard to admit but I see that I also feel important talking with you, as if the subject matter and your insights show that I am a substantial person. The thirst is more like a yearning but it's not only for the understanding. It's also to be a part of something I believe you represent. That feels uncomfortable. I don't like it. I think I should not desire it.

Ba: Why?

Q: It seems needy and I don't want to be perceived that way.

Ba: Why not?

Q: Oh. It's a violation of the way I was raised. Self-sufficiency and don't rely on anyone, if you want it done right, you will do it yourself, and on and on. That's what you mean by thoughts carrying the past into the future.

Ba: Yes. And the consequence of living by these thoughts?

Q: Loneliness. Oh, ow! It's skewed every one of my relationships! That's painful.

Ba: Self-inquiry has taken you to a block to self-knowledge that has been living in you. Seeing that, what will you do? It is a powerful moment. Can we not flinch as we participate in it? How can we not flinch?

The application of reflection and self-inquiry is central to transformation of old habits of thought. With self-inquiry we become aware of our assumptions, automatic responses, myths, assumed values and beliefs, explanations, and justifications that run our life as unquestioned norms.

Many of these unquestioned norms are passed down from generation to generation and frame our knowledge base of what we think makes life easy.

Self-inquiry is a way to avoid the unnecessary suffering that arises when we do not actualize our true nature and utilize all our capacities in life. We develop a sense of "self" that is free from the conditionings of the biographical past, with a good sense of discrimination and judgment, imbued with purpose, meaning, and intrinsic values.

Summing up, self-inquiry is:

- Honest, quiet, critical reflection on our own thoughts, actions, feelings, and motivations
- A form of experiential knowledge-of-the-self that transcends beliefs and offers moments in which insight can emerge
- A process that leads to increased awareness and self-knowledge whereby a core-self is uncovered

Self-knowledge cannot be given to you by anyone else. It must come from your own self-inquiry that examines taken-for-granted "truth" that stems from the past. Self-knowledge means "a turning of the personality," a making alive in the fullest sense of these words. It allows our reality to be seen and understood. With self-inquiry we become transparent to ourselves and thus enjoy freedom to make new choices.

But in not flinching, something deeper happens. We humans have the ability to know ourselves for who we truly are. What we perceive—the content of consciousness—is not who we are. Who perceives . . . is the question. If I am not the contents of my consciousness, then who am I?

If judgments and standards dissolve, what is left?

Two poems, to pay due homage to self inquiry:

Surrender

I surrender.
Resistance leads to exhaustion.
Concentration fills the eye of the needle.
Nothing passes through.

I cannot figure out five hundred billion galaxies
or the delight of relationship.
Every direction I look goes to infinity.
Every emotion I feel connects to eternity.
I surrender.

The mark of an awakened person is clear.
She will never claim origination.
For that would imply her death.

Musings from Consciousness and Beyond

I cannot stop nagging about this consciousness thing.
If you get it, you will be happy forever.
You will know love beyond-an-object.
But if you don't

Suffering will increase.
It's that simple.
I cannot mince words.

Attention on outcomes is misplaced.
Outcomes are just that—outcomes.
Why identify yourself as an outcome?
Are you your performance?
Your momentary emotion?
That thought?
(oh shit, the son-of-a-bitch just disappeared.)
Or your job?

Are you an accountant? A dancer?
Are you skinny? Rich?
Are you successful? Popular?
Are you smart? Well dressed?
Are you a Democrat? A Red Sox fan?
Are you a poet? A teacher?
An environmentalist? A spiritual leader?
Just who are you?
That's what I want to know.
Who are you?

Could you be the consciousness from which all this arises?

Could it be?

All the attempts to describe consciousness are vain
For consciousness is the source of the description.
Looking for consciousness in art or philosophy
Is like looking in the pond for the moon.
Or calling the wave the ocean.
Or thinking that relationship is about you and me
and not we.

(My incredible, darling, awakened wife just peeked over my shoulder,
Laughed and said this whole poetry thing should be called
"Musings from Consciousness and Beyond.")

Here is how prior consciousness is:
Arising directly from the unknowable
The progenitor of cascading spiraling DNA
The birthplace of epistemology
The unquestionable answer to all philosophy and religion
That shows that answers are the cosmetic for insecurity.
Only the unknowable lies beyond.

Chapter 2:
Who is the Self in Self-knowledge?

Ba: Ask the question: Who Am I?

Q: I have heard this question before and I can never wrap my mind around it.

Ba: We have established that we are not what we do, that our nature cannot be known by our behavior.

Q: Nature is another buzz word. Is the I of "Who Am I?" the same as our nature?

Ba: Nature means that which we are born with. It refers to our essence, the synergistic whole of our core qualities. Nothing is left out. Knowing our nature, we contact the meaning of our being, of our existence.
   Again I pose the question: Who Am I?

Q: I know that we have to start from ourselves. And I assume that by asking this question now you are working from the basis of self observation and selfinquiry. Are we embarking on your personal self-inquiry?

Ba: Yes and no. You ask an excellent question. It calls for a careful response. It is mine, and given the many people with whom I have worked and the research I have done, it applies to many. I prefer to talk about the commonalities. These rich descriptions have the widest applicability. If important, I will indicate differences with my personal inquiry.

For most of us, we believe that we are separate, that we have fallen or been born with bad karma or original sin and now must strive to regain wholeness. Wrong has been insidiously conflated with bad and so making a mistake has become proof of our moral corruption. The belief in separation becomes inevitable. We often believe we are broken.

Q: In other words, we judge ourselves.

Ba: Precisely. Self-knowledge has been reduced to self-consciousness. The judgment extends to praise as well as to blame and, most debilitating, to shame. As I started to self-observe, I saw that many of my thoughts centered on what I believed others thought of me. Self-inquiry revealed that most of my thoughts and actions aimed to actualize who I thought I should be. Deepening inquiry led to the painful realization that I had little knowledge of how or why I constructed this person. Who was I? I certainly hadn't made conscious or conscientious choices. Then the coup de grâce: I had no idea how I had come to think as I did. The very process of thinking itself became suspect. I was separated from the way I 'knew' myself.

Q: We judge ourselves because we have been judged since birth? Is that what you are saying? And that judgment has skewed all aspects of our lives, including the very way we perceive ourselves?

Ba: We must see this separation in ourselves to begin to appreciate self-knowledge. Skipping over it leads to belief in a struggle between light and dark. Self-knowledge is the light and the dark and beyond the light and the dark.

Attaching to the thought of separation and operating from it is the conventional way of living. Inquiring into this thought with all faculties is living self-knowledge. This dialogue is a version of that inquiry.

We start with self-observation. We start with who we are, not who we wish to be. Self-knowledge means to become intimate with ourselves as we are. It is not a means to get into heaven, to please a guru, to insure a better incarnation, to assuage guilt, to fight demons, to leave a "good" legacy, or for any other culturally created notion.

Inquiry is not only a thinking exercise. It is a full participation in the wholeness of the moment, including each feeling and event that glues us to the separation paradigm. Inquiry ends in clear perception.

Here's how this pernicious belief in separation plays out. Conditioned to believe in separation from birth, the fear arises of knowing ourselves as we are. Is it really true that all humans are by nature sinful and bad? Are we a morass of sludge at our core, without meaning or worth? The subtle shadow of questionable self-worth creeps in and haunts. We strive throughout our lives to prove we are worthwhile. We judge our worth by our performance. Exhaustion follows. Depleted, we doubt our ability to participate in self-inquiry. Traditional habits and rationalizations re-attach, perhaps more firmly than ever. "Ism's" form. Extrinsic validation replaces intrinsic knowing. Signs, symbols, and books codify "should."

Trying to make the ism's go away, or avoiding them, is a denial of self. It is the knowledge of self, and not the content of the knowledge, that affords liberation. All events and experiences are the fodder for self-knowledge.

This poem reflects my imprisonment in food-ism.

Food

I was a vegetarian for 22 years.
Guillotining countless cauliflowers, pulverizing billions of soy beans into tofu;
even eating the okara—now there's an intestinal freight train.

Piling huge amounts of shit
on small portions of Earth.
Earth never concentrated shit that way.

I fed scores from this labor.

Then my heart spoke.
Now I eat to live.

Conscience—the Necessary Foundation for Inquiry

This poem reflects upon my life in separation in my early teens.

Adolescence

As a 13-year-old I went golfing.
My playing partner became sick and left.
Alone on an unknown course.

As usual, I played terribly,
Wandering around after the ball
Berating myself for my ineptitude.

The huge course swallowed me.
I had no idea which fairway matched which green
As I trudged after slices and hooks.
Even with no one around
I lied about my score.

By the fourth hole
The humidity and my score passed 90.
Mosquitoes swarmed, nipping at my sweat-burning eyes.
Damp dungarees chafed my blubbery thighs
Crotch rot crawled
Into breast flab, neck flap, underarm crease.

Black and blue clouds blanketed the sky.
No wind, no breath.

Audibly chastising and exhorting myself
In alternating fits of anguish
With nothing left to lose
I stepped to the tee
and furiously blasted the ball.

I had heard that sound once before;
My one Little League home run.
Only this was clearer, purer, a glacier calving.
The ball soared, as if aching for the freedom to never stop.
White lightening stabbed the sky
Which answered with moaning cannon-thunder.

For moments the ball dissolved
As the lightening stabbed and stabbed.
Suddenly flickering into sight--
A white meteor against the plum purple sky.

At the zenith of its flight
The sun slid through a seam in the clouds.
Silent.
Glistening.
Emerald, sapphire, gold.
The end of time.

Salted mouth.
Rain mixed with sweat and tears.
Slogging back sopping,

Raw inside and out.

Q: I agree though the specifics of my experience were quite different. But I, and almost everyone I know, could sum up their teen experience as alienation, alienation, alienation.

Ba: Those folks who claim otherwise soon see it differently when practicing self-observation and self-inquiry. But I do want to hold out that some people were nurtured as teens. I know that freedom from alienation is possible because of my work in Natural Learning Relationships and the many children, families, and professionals I have worked with.

The following poem records an experience in self-observation in the presence of faux consciousness.

Right Speech

I surrendered to the green intoxication of the
Missouri River trail
And gently followed the conversation of my
companions.
It was talk about spirit,
But not spirit talk.
I didn't interrupt.
Intoxicated people say stupid things.

Even on this well-worn trail,

With the river altered like a Beverly Hills socialite
Reverence was the amrita of every breath.
The arthritis in my knees dissolved.
What is the epistemology of joy?

Companion X, Charlie by name, insisted I listen to
a story about the wisdom of his teacher.
I could not refuse.
Blake's right:
He who binds to himself a joy does the winged life destroy;
but he who kisses the joy as it flies lives in eternity's sun rise.
Life is living.

So I listened as Charlie told me that his teacher (an American with an Indian name who put new words to classic rock to convey his "anti-ego" message) told him that if he were negotiating between the Palestinians and the Jews, he would insist that they forgive one another and forgiveness was the answer if only people understood what true forgiveness was which Charlie explained was a feeling that really couldn't be explained and that too many words ruined the ambience in which forgiveness arises.

Whew!

Companion Y, Fred by name, asked my opinion of Charlie's exegesis.
Helpless, I shrugged.

And then it happened.
The path wound towards the river
And afforded a small plateau looking over a steep cliff.
Two men and a 10-year-old girl approached from the opposite direction.
We stepped aside to let them pass.
Delighted, the girl saw the plateau and skipped towards it.
Both men grabbed her arms.
"Good girls don't do that. They don't take chances."
With a slight push they moved her on her way.
I crumpled.
A mini smashed head-on by a semi.

The XY that is Charlie Fred continued walking talking.
They had seen what I had witnessed.
Arthritis everywhere now.
It's hard enough to reenter
Into the loving arms of my family.
To crash with these fools was a full-on bummer.

Chapter 2: Who is the Self in Self-knowledge?

> But I asked,
> "What do you think of the interaction of those men and that girl?"
> Blank. Vacant.
> So I told them what I thought of Charlie's teacher's ideas
> And I told of the coherence of spiritual philosophy
> And I drilled their hearts
> And I shone until I blinded them.
>
> Let the teacher pick up the pieces.
> He gets paid well, I'm sure.

Q: Were you angry?

Ba: Hurt. The combination of phony teacher, neglected child, and pseudo-spiritual blathering wounds. Hurt and then anger. Still am, though not about this specific incident. It has taken years of work to participate in my anger. Now it fuels creativity.

Q: What do you mean by participating in anger?

Ba: That's a big question and worthy of careful consideration. We will take it up shortly.

Q: But we are conversing about alienation. And you say that we are often blind to it. What do you mean?

Conscience—the Necessary Foundation for Inquiry

Ba: Many people attach to what they do rather than who is doing it. At that moment they lose contact with their motivations and self knowledge. This alienates even when the activity seems beneficial and has social approval.

This poem talks of alienation masking social approval.

Green

Oh yeah, I knew this guy,
An environmental activist in a rural community.
He wrote the legal briefs that saved endangered species.

I mean I really knew him.
He was good to look with
Keen observant listening
And generous.

We made money together and laughed about it.
His children loved me
But his wife didn't.
She was green, but in a different way.

It went south overnight;
A one wayer, no roundtrip.
Yeah, her toxic gossip ate hearts
But his pollution, when I saw it, was worse.

> Children need their parents
> More than briefs.
> An insane price for nobility.
> The violence of fractured relationship.

Conscience—the Necessary Foundation for Inquiry

Ba: To do this, to inquire into the nature of self, requires a healthy conscience.

Q: You are talking about how to tell good from bad. But that is judgment. So healthy conscience, given what what's been said, seems like an oxymoron.

Ba: A healthy conscience simply allows all the feelings in the moment to be present, without filter, avoidance, or attraction. At times, the feelings may contradict one another. Still, we must feel all the feelings without judgment. This is what I meant by participation when we spoke earlier about my participation in my anger.

This is a new way of knowing conscience. It is not good vs. bad. It is not the perversion that results in guilt and shame. This conscience is our naturally functioning capacity, a quality of our wholeness. The only block to our actualization of healthy conscience is the pernicious conditioned habit imposed upon us, and used to control us, of judgment—of good vs. bad, of shame and blame, or sin and penance.

Q: You are going to have to explain this. I have never heard this before.

Ba: Feeling all of our feelings without judgment enhances the rich texture of existence and reveals the wisdom inherent in human emotions. A loved one dies and there is gratitude for the time shared and sadness at the loss. A divorce occurs and there is relief, anger, concern, loneliness, freedom, doubt, and renewal. They are all there, though in different proportions for different people in different circumstances. The simple function of conscience is to feel them all, as they are, as they arise.

Q: It sounds like you are saying that the pain and suffering of divorce is okay, that they are balanced, or mitigated, by the other feelings.

Ba: No. To do so makes an ordeal such as divorce bad or wrong which then needs to be remedied. Nor am I glorifying divorce, or any ordeal. The words *order* and *ordeal* share the same root. We have the potential to make order out of ordeals. Nor am I suggesting that actualizing conscience buffers the suffering in an ordeal. I am pointing the way to self-knowledge.

We can make this clear by inquiring directly into the suffering that religions contend permeates the human condition.

Religion and Conscience

Q: It's canon that the dominant religions agree that to be born as a human is the result of a negative catastrophe, such as a fall, bad karma, or sin. All of their efforts, therefore, are to heal this terrible wound, to atone, to free the mind of harmful thoughts or feelings, to "pay" for the right to a life free from suffering.

Ba: In an attempt to heal this supposed wound, religions pervert conscience to simplistic notions of good and bad. That way people can "pay" with good acts and atone for bad ones. This insult to our natural capacity to feel all the feelings has long-lasting disastrous ramifications. It's like reducing cognitive capacities to associative thinking, rather than including concentration, reflexive contemplation, and inspiration. It's like reducing the body to eating, defecating, breathing, and desires.

Religions vary in their myths of how this catastrophe occurred but the proof that it has is the inevitable fact of each individual's suffering. It is not considered that the suffering may be generated by the *thought* of the "fall" and the subsequent adherence to the rituals and status hierarchies needed to maintain the religious institutions—those self-same religious institutions that generate and perpetuate the attachment to notions of recovering grace. It is not considered that there is necessary suffering and unnecessary suffering and that the necessary suffering may in fact be a weave in the fabric of our greatness and wholeness while the unnecessary suffering perpetuates itself through shame and guilt about an imagined sin.

Q: But suffering is real. We all suffer. Why wouldn't we want an end to suffering? Religious rituals and institutions don't seem too high a price to pay for a response to suffering.

Ba: When suffering is allowed to just be, without attributing cause and trying to react to the attribution, its inherent value can be perceived. The revelation is simple: Unnecessary suffering arises from ignorance. Necessary suffering, such as that which arises with the death of a loved one, yields meaning and stimulates intimate relationships. Necessary suffering is nothing less than the medium for profound learning about love. This does not mitigate the feelings of sadness and yearning. It does end resistance to death and to nature. It allows for an infant's vulnerability in each of us. Necessary suffering unmitigated by thought of separation yields infinite gratitude at the opportunity to love.

Therefore, suffering is not proof of separation, of sin, or of any other construct that holds that humans are not inherently whole. We exist; we are human beings. That is the fruit of a healthy conscience inquiring into self and suffering.

Poems about Conscience

Every Emotion Counts

Whatever you worry about you adore.
Whatever you envy you worship.
Rage is your thirst for justice.
Lust cries out for union.
Fear shouts for communion.
Greed begs for equality.
Aggression attempts self-protection.

Every emotion counts.
Well-being is inexorable
Composting the confusions
Creating the rich soil in which the seed of self-knowledge grows.
Spirituality is never not here.

I am ruined for acting in this world
For I refuse to compete to be heard.

Impartiality and Bitterness

The guru-driven ethic of the religious community:
"Make eye contact and smile."
Which, as the sexual harassment conviction suggests,
He did perfectly well.

Religion and Conscience

It cost millions.
They decided to clear-cut their trees,
to compromise their watershed,
to uglify their home,
to disrespect their neighbors,
to leave the world worse for their children who,
they insisted, must make eye contact and smile.

I can't say it often enough.
The only way out is through.
Bitterness has its purpose.
Impartiality is the enduring residue of emotional participation.

Watch.

Without censorship, feel this:

An aged ex-Nazi ruling millions of Catholics,
rich beyond imagination.
condemning other religions,
ordering poor people to have children they cannot support,
vilifying homosexuals,
covering up child rapists,
excommunicating activist priests,
denigrating women,
ignoring the environment,
killing in the name of his Savior,

and telling you how to drive a car about which,
like sex, he knows nothing.

A Crusader President,
rich in dollars and goodwill Democracy.
spending it on torture,
ignoring Darfur,
mythologizing science,
rationalizing killing,
justifying torture,
running a shadow government,
ignoring the environment,
sacrificing the poor to the wealthy,
fealty obsessed,
surrounded by henchman,
and telling you how to educate children about which,
like spirituality, he knows nothing.

Don't reject, rationalize, or rearrange the bitterness.
Don't react or argue.
Let its heat eat any helplessness.

An ancient wisdom arises.
Unremitting empathy.
Stainless intention to spin the chakra
And end unnecessary suffering.
Impartiality in the midst of life.

So, instead of wishing ill of the guru, the pope, and the president
You might ask:
Sri Guru: Are the women that you abused making eye contact and smiling?
Your Holiness the Pope: How many Hail Mary's did you have to say to gain absolution for the murder of a million gypsies, all the Jews, and was there extra penance for the Catholics that that Nazi has murdered? And how many Our Fathers will it take to atone for the predator priests who destroyed the lives of so many children?
Mr. President: Which is tougher to live with? The action that led tens of thousands of Americans and Iraqis to their deaths, or the lack of action that led tens of thousands of Darfur citizens to their deaths?

Honest questions, freely asked.
No answer required.

Separation, Perfection, Alienation, Compensation

Q: I have read in several Eastern philosophies that the body is the problem. Therefore the thought "I am my body" is a fundamental belief in separation. The thought then arises that I have to overcome my separation, which is rooted in my body. As bodies are the natural condition of birth, both bodies and nature become obstacles to self-knowledge. I don't agree but have to admit that each of us has our own body and that, in part, we know ourselves by identifying with the body.

Ba: Is the problem with the body or with the identification? What if having a body is not bad or proof of some ontological wrong-doing? What if the confusion is the *thought* that birth in a body is the bad karma? What if there is really nothing to overcome, that each life is whole and worthwhile in all its moments of existence? What if existence is its own liberation and we only need the false thoughts dissolved to know that?

Q: Are you implying that the problem is the identification, whether with the body or anything else?

Ba: What does it mean to identify? How did it occur in you? Those are the questions. Pinning the problem on the object of the identification is as mistaken as believing that your achievements define who you are. I know that I have said it before, and I will probably say it again: It is self-knowledge and not the contents of knowledge that is the sacred human gift.

Q: Are there other consequences of belief in separation?

Ba: The thought of separation is generalized into the ideal of perfection. Having fallen, there is the need to return to perfection. With no functional relationship to suffering, there must be perfection to save us. With conscience reduced to polarized good and bad, there must be perfection. Without development of the natural capacity to deal with feelings of inadequacy, helplessness, and fear, there must be perfection.

The notion of perfection is not only silly but an obvious compensation for feelings of inadequacy and insecurity. In an evolving emergent world, perfection can only be imposed.

This leads to insidious, pernicious unnecessary suffering. If we are born bad and fallen into separation and now must seek perfection to achieve order, then life is an endless seeking, an endless feeling of inadequacy, an endless attempt to overcome insecurity. The psychological response is compensation and alienation. They really are one and the same. Alienated from our wholeness we seek compensation in addictions.

Q: What do you mean by addiction? It is a dirty word in our world. Addicted people hurt themselves and others. They are to be avoided, preferably institutionalized.

Ba: Addiction is using an activity or an event or a relationship to attempt to fulfill the hole left when we stop trusting our wholeness. Anything to prove our worth. Anything to prove we are not bad. If our baseball team wins, we are lucky. If we wear the right clothes, we are acceptable. If we have the appropriate orgasms, we are potent. If we have inner experiences of peace and light, we are special. If we have degrees from universities, we are smart. If we have lots of money, we are potent and smart and lucky and special and very acceptable.

When we don't find the specialness in ourselves, we identify with others who seem special. This childish transference is everywhere and is the unmistakable sign of the exhaustion of people who have spent their whole lives trying to overcome the thought of their separation, of trying to perform to perfection. This hero worship extends to actors, politicians, religious leaders, athletes, and artists. It is most obvious when the hero is also famous, but fame is not a requirement as the transference is to the role, not to the person. That is why the people fulfilling the role dress and act the part. We would not look up to the neighborhood priest if he did not wear his robes and his fancy costume for special masses.

Q: I am beginning to see how fundamentally flawed the belief in separation is.

Ba: There's more. Addiction to perfection is one of the worst of all addictions. As a corrupted conscience preoccupied with good vs. bad can never attain perfection, the addiction is extended into the afterlife. There, after death, we will find perfection. Whoa! Without one shred of direct evidence, the belief in a perfect afterlife persists. Could there be any clearer indicator of the wound of separation than the compensatory belief in a perfect afterlife?

Q (smiling): That's true. Real estate in heaven is the most expensive real estate there is.

Ba: Belief in separation is ingrained in the zeitgeist—in the prevalent ideas dominating our time. For example, most of the charitable work in society is directed at the wounds that the separation has caused. These efforts only partially succeed for they fail to see and address the root of the problem. Some of these efforts make things worse by giving the false impression that something is being done about the problem and thus valuable resources are being misappropriated. At some point, attention must be turned to the basic psychological need to know ourselves without blame, shame, and culturally imposed expectations. At some point, children must not be so harshly conditioned to cultural norms and goals but appreciated and supported in fulfilling their own destinies. There are some notable attempts to do this throughout history by self-knowledgeable people, but they are the rare exception.

Three Aspects of Self

Q: Can you sum up this inquiry into self-knowledge?

Ba: (Laughing). Only as a sketch. Each of us has to fill in the details.

Humanity has three basic distinguishing qualities of self. By basic, I mean a set of characteristics, attributes, and capacities. There are many variations on each, so be careful.

Without your own self- inquiry, this could be taken as a template, or as a definitive answer.

The identified conditioned self—the self who holds the thought of separation, the addicted self, the self who glimpses the reality of separation and turns away, the self who cynically pledges allegiance to ism's while hypocritically acting against his or her stated convictions, the self dependent on extrinsic direction, the self who feels blamed, judged, and victimized and compensates by exploiting or by idolizing the underdog—is me.

Me is possessive, primarily concerned by biological drives (sex, food, territorial defense of physical and psychological boundaries) and sees self-knowledge as extraneous to "the real world."

Q: You make it sound awful.

Ba: Left on its own it is awful. But under the aegis of the other selves, me serves physical survival and many of the mundane tasks I–and everyone else–must perform. It is ancient, and like the organs in our body, necessary.

Q: Who are these other selves?

Ba: The self who accepts meaning as intrinsically important, who has some sense that religion is really about spirituality, who doubts and inquires, who is drawn to greater inclusiveness, who sees change as the necessary evolutionary agent for greater emergence and self-knowledge—is I.

I accepts the psyche as the meeting ground of reality. I analyzes. I measures, compares, and creates systems. I knows that there are different modes of knowing, different ways of organizing self, life, and the universe. This fills I with great wonder, humility, motivation, and humor.

I creates the demand for a uniform way of measuring all describable and designable systems. In response to this demand, I uses time as a variable and so creates systems that challenge and change perception. Computers and evolutionary theory are two examples of I at work.

Q: I sounds great. Are there no problems with it?

Ba: Captivated by the power and breathtaking perspectives made available through its invention of time, I often forgets who invented it. Then hubris moves in. Thought is venerated. When thought rules, emotions are reduced to timed chemical processes; self either ends at death or is relegated to fantasy (in the sense of non-verifiable) realms of heaven/hell or reincarnation; non-thought realities are believed to be imagined or discounted as unimportant or available only to a select few. Words and concepts rule. Science is conflated with truth. Education is defined by verbal-linguistic and logical mathematical testing.

When not ensnared by hubris, I brings its prodigious powers to inquiry and dialogue. When that inquiry is turned inward, then self-knowledge becomes a possibility.

Q: I am not sure I understand. This summary has turned into generalizations. Can you be more specific?

Ba: Let's turn to some poems that describe aspects of each of these two selves.

Here is a poem of Me struggling:

Symbiosis

Did Obama thank Bush
For being such a fuck-up
That he made it easy to be elected?
Do the muck-racking sports journalists thank the steroid-bloated athletes
For the many meals their asininities provide?
Do cops thank criminals
Or priests thank sinners?
Sometimes, it's challenging to recognize friends.
We all eat one another.
What is the boundary between ambition and greed?

These poems are I at play:

If I Were A Painting...

You could paint the canvas of my life cubistically

Or surreally or expressionistically or abstractly or
minimistically or just paint the whole thing white
Or leave it blank.
But no pop art please;
No time freedom there.

Chronological renderings mislead
By concretizing consciousness into past present
and future
When past present and future are but one child of
consciousness.

I Seem to be a Meme

I seem to be a meme.
Legomonism.
Agent of the Collective Unconsciousness.
Translator of the Akashic records.
Dancer from the Evolutionary future.
Terma carrier.

How is it that you see?
How is it that you perceive?
How is it that you know?
Start there.
The rest will follow.
Did you really believe that freedom was the right
to vote?

I am Poetry

I am poetry.
Meaning and care
drenching every breath, every word.
As much as I love you
I can only snatch fragments.

Every poem, every line, every word,
pulls in nine directions.
North, east, south, west, up, down, in, out,
And empty-silent-nowhere.

You cannot name that which is ineffable.
That is not poetry's purpose.
You cannot make words beautiful.
Trying dams the flow.
No poetry will awaken Love,
Nor pretend towards Truth,
Nor inspire Devotion,
Nor quell Fear, or end Insecurity.

Poetry is what remains
When all these aspirations dissolve.

Q: And the third self?

Ba: There aren't really three selves. Each is an aspect of self-knowledge. That is a wisdom of the third aspect of self.

When the inquiry is fully done, when perception is self-knowledge and separation has been clearly seen—i exists. i is the self that transmutes addiction into passion, allegiance into freedom, blame into compassion. i includes all feelings without judgment or prejudice. i does not seek liberation, does not think about liberation any more than most parents question their love for their child. Liberation is i's natural state.

i is simultaneously whole and emergent. Realization of this quality ends all chauvinism for no one is complete and no one is incomplete. i fills out the person according to his or her capacities and talents in that moment of life.

i responds to need. Need is an active force in the river of creativity that runs through all existence. i requires no effort to recognize need and complete freedom when responding to it.

Q: This use of need needs explaining.

Ba: Indeed it does for it is central to self-knowledge. Trust me for now. Let your intuition as to what I mean by need guide you for the moment. We will come back to it.

Q: Just so you know, my intuitive understanding suggests that by linking need, creativity, and self-knowledge, you are intimating purpose and direction in life and the Universe. Further, that only through self-knowledge can we know how this lives in us.

Ba: Fair enough.

i's freedom often challenges all the me and I identities. i has no need for goddesses and gods, for Earth Mothers and Sky Fathers, for spiritual metaphors, for external judges or judgment days, for commandments or parables, for philosophies about the nature of life, or for systems that rationalize the gestalt of relationship.

i has no unnecessary fears. i protects the body and those relationships that serve self-knowledge.

Q: So we only need i?

Ba: Humans are me, I, and i. Setting one against another is just another separation illusion. Truly, living as I has greater tolerance, perspective, and enjoyment in relationship than does living as me. Learning is faster, more complete, and alive with incisive curiosity. Living as I satisfies me's needs. There is no loss of security, or reproductive energy, or appropriate boundaries. However, it could as well be said that a healthy me lives under the aegis of I and quietly attends to the needs it recognizes. There is no need to theorize or try to prove distinctions. There is only observation, inquiry, and appreciation of well-being and wholeness.

Self-knowledge allows me, I, and i to blend into a harmonious whole that is greater than any of them. Wildly unpredictable, that whole defies description. It is for each of us to discover for ourselves. It is the great journey of life, the sacredness of each breath and the redemption of all suffering, both necessary and unnecessary.

Poems Hinting at Liberation:

When Selfishness Ends

I begin when selfishness ends.
Floating on gratitude for all the people in my life
A land of self-discovery.

Did you ever dream what it would be like to have:
- dzogchen without Buddhism
-Christ without guilt
-prayer liberated from petition
-democratic gurus
-and only chosen people.
Religion selfishly binds spiritual technologies.
You don't really need Tara or Mary
To know devotion.

I know that I know
That i am.
It is sufficient.

Happiness

The only true—that is, beyond pleasure and pain—
happiness
Arises with self-knowledge.

When you know yourself, you will know the laws of
the universe.
You will know all that can be known
And all that cannot.
Both will surprise you.
Quietly you will know what has been in your bones
since before the beginning
Before the before
And before that.
The argument ends
And the questions come to life.
Living these paradoxes is freedom.

Miracle

Nature's Laws are always and everywhere.
Why this interest in supposed miracles
When you are the wonder of the world?

Chapter Three:
On Relationship, Conscience, and Self-knowledge

Q: I am a person who loves life. I especially enjoy close relationships. Yet, when I consider what you have said about conscience, I see that I am not "feeling all the feelings," as you put it. My way with people is to think about what I feel and what they say and do and then, if it is positive, to try to connect with them. I am concerned that accessing conscience will get in my way.

Ba: Every relationship serves self-discovery. Inevitably, relationship is learning about ourselves. It does not matter how or why the relationship began or what we believe fuels its continuation. Family, sex, fun, mutual interests, business, circumstances, or chance may be the way things begin or the medium in which they reoccur, but the fact remains that any and all human-to-human encounters factor into emergent self-awareness.

Q: *Every* relationship?

Ba: We learn as much about ourselves by what we reject as what we accept. We create boundaries through what we allow as much as through what we disallow. It is this learning that furthers self-knowledge. Self-observation and conscience provide the medium for this learning to occur.

Q: That means no judgment.

Ba: Relationship teaches each of us about ourselves. Judging a relationship is a twisted way of saying what we are learning about ourselves. To say that someone is bad is to say that you found their actions harmful to you. It therefore reveals your vulnerability to that type of harm. To say that others are lesser because of race, gender, or status is to say that you need special protection from some sort of fear and that these are the chosen barriers. To say someone is great or wonderful is to say that they bring forth what you believe are healthy feelings and attributes. To say that another acted in the appropriate manner reveals your expectations of social justice.

These interpersonal events are data by which we come to know ourselves. If awareness stops at the judgment, then ignorance prevails and learning occurs in slow, brutish ways. This is unnecessary suffering. Humans do not need to oppress one another in order to prove they are right, that another is bad, their morals are superior, their status higher, or their religion better. Each attempt to do so ignores the fact that the value of the relationship is what it teaches us about ourselves. In the act of projection, self-awareness disappears. The other becomes the focus and the lens that you see them through is justified instead of examined. Why do

"I" see them that way? What does seeing them that way say about "me"? How did I come to see them that way? Do I have confidence in that mode of seeing?

Participating in these questions takes the judgment out of the relationship. All relationships have value. All are meaningful. All bring forth and reflect an aspect of ourselves. Typical of humans, when there is no new learning, boredom descends. The relationship then either transforms, in which new discoveries occur, or it ends. The end of relationship means that learning no longer occurs or that habit, born out of conditioning and never questioned, runs the show.

Q: So there are different kinds of relationships. But you are saying that what glues us to the relationship is the quality of learning involved. What about love, or at least affinity?

Ba: Love is a special case that we will consider later and in great detail. I think you will find it surprising. And yes, affinity is a function of learning. Recall the trajectory of affinities that you have had in life. Did you believe in everlasting love with your first romantic engagement? Perhaps, like me, you had rapport with a professor as well as a mutual interest in an academic subject. In my case, I believed we would be working together for a long time, but it only lasted three years. Each of us has similar experiences. Very few affinities endure.

Q: Sure, but interests change, people move, stuff happens.

Ba: That's the point. Affinities have duration. That duration is based on learning. Have any of your affinities survived the changes in your life?

Q: Yes. Okay, yes, and it is accurate to say they lasted due to mutual interest. But the endings of others have often been painful. Why painful, if the interest has lagged?

Ba: The end of a relationship always brings new learning, some of it difficult to digest. A multitude of feelings descend, many of them contradictory. Hurt, anger, disappointment eat us alive, especially where there has been strong affinity and care. How could I have done more? Where did it go wrong? Why wasn't my love reciprocated? How do I deal with this ache of loneliness, this tidal wave of insecurity, this feedback that I am a miserable or inadequate person? And, what is wrong with him/her/them that they have turned into such jerks? Why didn't I see it sooner? What is their problem? What is my problem? What is the problem? All of this is just another way of saying that there are parts of yourself that you do not know. It is not intimacy with the other that is lacking but intimacy with yourself. Shadows creep in, subtle self-righteousness appears in the middle of the night; you realize that all sorts of supposed knowledge was merely assumption. Hurt and anger at the stupidity of not seeing it coming is to curse our own blindness. Who the hell am I anyway? Why don't I have the skills I need? Where did I learn what relationship is and what it is supposed to be? How can I know what I don't know about?

Only healthy conscience can help. Only the ability to sit with all the feelings without flinching can stimulate those inner faculties that can assimilate the data and transform it into self-knowledge. As difficult as it may seem at the time, that information, that intense stream of feelings is the heat that turns the garbage of the thoughts of separation into the soil in which inherent self-knowledge flourishes. The way out uses the material of the confusion itself. There is no place to go but home to ourselves, because home is where it has always been.

Q: You are positing relationship as sacred, as part of a spiritual path. That seems a reach to me. I can see that I really don't want so much weight given to relationships. They are a time of relaxation and enjoyment for me.

Ba: Nowhere in any of our dialogue am I talking about a spiritual path. My part in our dialogue is testimony from the realm of self-knowledge.

Relationship is about self-discovery. We engage one another and the world to know ourselves, which speaks to great admiration and respect for all relationships. In a completely non-narcissistic way, we long to know ourselves and so we turn every event, relationships included, to that end. Sitting with conscience requires great effort. Since birth, there has been the same message over and over: we are separate individuals who must regain our wholeness. Stained by some unknown sin, our well-meaning parents and guardians reduced conscience to the "norms" of right/wrong, good/bad, me/not-me. With no mentoring to feel all the feelings, we approach relationship with similar superficial dichotomies such as like/dislike, pretty/ugly, my religion/not my religion.

Q: Since it begins in childhood, should we look there for a remedy?

Ba: Yes. Nurturing conscience in children would eliminate the unnecessary suffering, and pain in relationship would dissolve into the great expanse of self-knowledge.

This poem talks of one benefit of conscientious relationship:

The End of Rejection

Imagine living without the fear of rejection,
Or the burden of rejecting others.
This is your world.
Yours and yours alone.
Immiscible.
Yet, integrated.

Q: The misunderstanding of the nature of conscience is insidious. Just how far does it go?

Ba: The perversion of conscience cripples the ability to realize self-knowledge. It is a heinous crime and repeatedly perpetrated on children. The absence of genuine conscience poisons personal, social, institutional, and political life. All other "solutions" to these species-threatening problems will continue to fail until a cadre of responsible people accesses conscience.

Q: Have you traced how the infection spreads?

Ba: A principal mechanism for perpetuating the perversion of conscience states that good things happen to good people and bad things happen to bad people. This pernicious lie reaches such lows as suggesting that those who suffer illness, or get mangled in an accident, or die in wars they did not start have done something wrong and are bad. For instance, children who die of starvation have bad karma but because they suffered their fate, they will be reborn into a better life or will be welcomed in "heaven" where, we assume, they will have enough to eat. It plays out in grandiose ways that leave us cringing with the absurdity of its claims such as "God is on our side so we will win the war." And this slavery-inducing belief is often used to excuse the lies and perfidy of the rich and famous. How can they be bad if they have so much power and wealth? How can they be bad when they must have been so right to gain so many good things?

A second and seemingly more sophisticated mechanism relies on the ubiquitous human trait to use thought to rationalize feelings. When there is hurt due to rejection or "failure" (in quotes here because success and failure are culturally constructed and entirely subjective), thoughts tend to jump in and buffer the pain.

Q: Be specific. How does this buffering occur?

Ba: For example, we experience a series of failures, and then use the story of how Abraham Lincoln lost every election until the Presidency. We rationalize our own suffering with the thought that others are "worse off." Esoteric personality systems that claim to describe human types, such as the enneagram, or to describe our fate, such as astrology, are interpreted to "explain" how failure occurred. As a last resort, socially sanctioned resignation, found in clichés such as "it's God's will," or "life's not fair," or "you win some, you lose some," buffers the pain. These are thoughts, not feelings, and buffering the pain does nothing to alleviate unnecessary suffering or to access self-knowledge.

Moreover, and of great importance, no one has just one feeling at a time. When thought emphasizes one feeling and then rationalizes it, the synergy of feeling all the feelings without mitigation or modification never manifests. You never know yourself as emotionally wise.

Your spouse has an affair and lies about it. You find out. You are hurt, then angry. Thought rationalizes the anger. You are the victim of cheating and lying. Other emotions are neglected, such as embarrassment within your social circle, relief from the pressure of upholding a failing partnership, liberation from the bonds of a promise made that you no longer want to keep, fear of the future, helplessness, and perhaps a kind of happiness that your partner took the action that caused the crises. Congratulations! You are so deserving of sympathy—and so bereft of emotional wisdom.

Q: Painfully, I see these patterns in myself. I don't want to believe that I am emotionally immature. I want to believe that I did feel all the feelings. But I can see that I brushed over them.

Ba: Neglecting non-emphasized feelings weakens the inner moral and ethical faculties. It sets the conditions for self perceptions such as victim, morality enforcer, and the many other narcissistic and self-righteous behaviors. You know the morality enforcers. They are so sure they are right, good, and the defenders of the public purity. No one could be a morality enforcer if they felt the full body and texture of all their feelings for even one moment.

Q: For example?

Ba: Look at the way that fraud is rationalized. With a wearisome disingenuousness, those with corrupted consciences express surprise and outrage when fraud occurs. Yet fraud proliferates systemically in all cultural institutions, from perverted priests to thieving businessman to corrupt politicians. Shame about feeling fraudulent or feeling helpless obscures the truth that these feelings are natural to being a human. When accepted in healthy conscience, these feelings yield valued relationship insights that deepen intimacy, caring, and compassion.

Confession and penance, common in one form or another to every religion, have proved to be two great rationalizing thoughts. Speaking something out loud by rote and formula dulls the force of the feeling. It places the responsibility for the response for the supposed sin on the institution and its priest and fosters dependence on external guidance. As the feeling still lives within us, compensations such as sports, non-intimate sex, Disneyland-type fun, and other mind-numbing activities are used to keep the feelings at bay.

With deadly dependability, rationalizing feelings results in people not taking control where they can and trying to control what they cannot. Obvious venues of self-control, such as diet and body shape, are given over to "experts" despite the common knowledge that there is a new diet every week and cultural ideals of the body change regularly.

Q: Part of me wants you to stop. It's just too far-reaching. I think I would rather hear about global warming.

Ba: A culture can be defined by the feelings that thought tends to emphasize over and over and the feelings that thought denies. For instance, in an individualistic (capitalistic) society, helplessness is repeatedly denied and the rationalizations come fast and furious when it is felt. You can see this in the pride a nation takes in its weapons. Gaudy displays of might is an attempt to mask insecurity. Why spend so many resources on weaponry that become obsolete quickly? Why pretend that the showing of great power overwhelms enemies when it usually helps them to devise new strategies (Viet Nam? Afghanistan?) Parading strength is intended to bolster confidence in the citizenry. Does your confidence increase due to these displays? Do they work? What is their attraction?

Q: The carnage of the 20th century proves your point. The arms race led to death. Their attraction is the sense of security they intend. When I self-observe, I feel the fear of someone trying to harm me. A vague anxiety haunts me; I believe I need protection.

This poem reflects the confusion attendant to rationalization:

Savior?

OK, let me get this straight.
Global warming, terror,
Mythic power gamblers running the show
And the Internet is going to save us?

Wait, wait, I'm supposed to believe that
Systemic prejudice, fat CEOs, and starving children
Will be ended by legislation?
Or the moral authority of the Church?

I get it; I'll just close my eyes
The Yankees are playing the Cowboys
(Did you see the slo-mo replay on my 60" plasma?)
And wait for the angels to save me.

> Who can participate in the pain?
> The only way out is through
> The answer lies within the problem
> You are that which you seek.

Q: My instinct is to avoid pain, not participate in it.

Ba: Is the pain external to you? Is someone or something causing you the pain?

Q: Obviously. I wouldn't hurt myself.

Ba: Why does it hurt?

Q: Might be physical, might be emotional. This seems obvious and a bit trivial.

Ba: Stick with me. Moving away from physical pain is obvious. Our dialogue at the moment centers on relationship, and relationship is an emotional event.

Q: It is. And yes, responding to the pain is picking out the dominant emotion.

Ba: Why did you?

Q: The pain is so strong it cannot be ignored.

Ba: Who decided on its strength? Who gave it that power?

Q: I did.

Ba: My simple suggestion is to feel all the feelings, then see how the pain lives in you. We have so many judgments around emotional pain and relationship.

Q: As a society, it certainly doesn't help to avoid the suffering. The problems just multiply and grow more intense.

Ba: How does our society view pain?

Q: As the enemy, as something to be defeated.

Ba: Has it worked?

Q: No, it's only so much wasted effort. In fact, it has had the opposite effect. There is more pain and confusion as evidenced in all we have said so far.

Ba: Most ethical matters derive their meaning from the situation in which they arise, the situations we are living at that moment. The best response can only be known in relationship to all that comprises that moment.

Q: In other words, memory play tricks and rationalizations creep in.

Ba: Sure. Have you had a broken romance?

Q: Yes.

Ba: In the moment of the break-up did you feel all the feelings?

Q: No, I went numb. I froze.

Ba: As so many of us do. Later, guilt often sets in. We believe we should have acted differently, said something, done something, anything...but numb.

Q: And if I felt all the feelings then, would there be no guilt later on?

Ba: You have to find out for yourself. For me, remorse arises without guilt as I replay that break-up moment.

Q: What is the difference between remorse and guilt?

Ba: Remorse is free of judgment. Remorse connects with the blindness, allows the helplessness, accepts responsibility for self-discovery, and leaves me open to new learning. The heat of remorse slowly composts the lies I told myself in order to miss the distance in the relationship.

Q: I see that for me the feeling of failure quickly morphs into numbness.

Ba: The speed of that transition reveals how quickly we leave the feelings of the moment and revert to cultural voices.

Q: By which you mean the unacceptability of failure and helplessness?

Ba: In this case, yes. To give away your power and control to a belief or a norm—reveals how constriction and fear have encased conscience and crippled the ability to respond.

At the same time people who lack a healthy conscience often become absorbed with events beyond their control. They try to control other people, or nature, or other nations, or other minds.

Once genuine conscience is activated, nothing else needs to be done. Humans have the inherent faculty to turn data into meaning; the purer the data, the more coherent the meaning. The evidence of this faculty is evident in every human-created system from philosophy to accounting to science. Ultimately no one knows how this occurs. No one disputes that it does. Conscience is the agent that transports the feeling-data to the meaning maker that lives in each of us, as each of us. With trust in ourselves—hard to do when separation has been hammered in since birth—and appreciation of the miracle of meaning-making, we can allow all the feelings to be present.

This is the genuine miracle of being. Mysterious, non-interfering, non-active yet continually providing the medium that necessitates dynamic emergence, being requires only participation without filters, without prejudice, without achievement. Being is simply natural sanity, well-being, and wholeness.

This poem sings of conscientious relationship:

This is Us, Me, We, I, and You

The mobilization against carbon emissions
Proves William James right
(See The Moral Equivalent of War)
Humans need frontiers to transcend.
It's the way we learn.

James picked the wrong object.
Overcoming nature is ridiculous;
It means overcoming yourself.
Balance with nature seems much better.
But it still falls short.
We pollute because we believe ourselves separate.
Because we are trapped in a mind-set that believes
we operate on a world out there.
Because we have lost the unity of mind and nature,
Because deep down we have not transcended the
conceits of original sin and bad karma,
And have not accepted our birthright as the rightful heirs
To Beauty, Love, and Truth.

How can we transcend the illusion of separation?

Chapter Three: On Relationship, Conscience, and Self-knowledge

By meeting the being needs of children.
Surprised?
No one has an "I-am-separate" gene.
Separation is learned.
Those who teach separation to children
Are the harbingers of doom.

Meeting the being needs of children
Means connected people.
Connected people don't pollute.
Because they would be polluting themselves.

You, too, will know wholeness
By nourishing the being needs of children.
Wholeness is infectious, our natural state.
Ever-blooming as the seed of time.

So easily the illusion shatters.
Heart armor crumbles.
Veils dissolve.
Finally, we see ourselves in one another, as one
another.
No more myths.
No more rationalizations of aloneness.
No more justifications of wounding.
We are the world.
I am the world.
This is us, me, we, I, and you.

Finally, we have taken responsibility for our minds,
For our species mind.
Finally, relational freedom
Emergent; self-knowledge; no fear.
There is only one frontier left.
And we are it.
Welcome.

Chapter Four:
On Meaning

Q: Earlier you said that meaning emerges from self-observation and self-inquiry. Now you have added conscience and conscientious relationship. Can we inquire into meaning directly?

Ba: We must; meaning draws us. Through meaning we organize our lives.

Q: How?

Ba: Let's slow down. We have to do take a look at evolution.

Q: I study evolutionary theory. It interests me.

Ba: What is your understanding of the relationship between meaning and evolution?

Q: I don't have a firm opinion. But I do know that the physical evolutionists call meaning an *epiphenomenon*. They claim it is a side result of the struggle to survive, and specifically for reproductive rights.

Ba: That's classic Darwinian Theory.

Q: You don't agree?

Ba: Darwin was close but he missed the essential human need for meaning. Without considering meaning, Darwinian Theory insists on morphological, physiological, and behavioral attributes. But humans need meaning. We search for it, sacrifice for it, worship it, impose it on others, and form civilizations around it.

Humans are drawn to meaning, but they are driven by the attributes that Darwin proselytized. Bull sea lions in heat are driven to find their beautiful cows. They are driven to eat, to secure their boundaries, and to reproduce. But draw is different. Like drive, draw is inherent and exerts an inexorable influence, whether recognized or not. Once recognized, however, draw gains immeasurable power in shaping our life. When we know that we are drawn to find meaning, then we begin to question the meaning value of all actions.

Q: What is the relationship between the drives and the draw?

Ba: Inquiry into meaning extends to the whole of our life. Therefore, fulfilling drives is now considered in light of their meaning. For example, analysis of food production, distribution, and consumption is rife with meaning. Corn has a different meaning for a Hopi than for an ethanol maker. No act, not even the most fundamental drive, can be viewed outside of the context of the draw of meaning. Drive cannot satisfy the draw, but draw will always satisfy the drive. Sex, for example, is more attractive, more empowering, and more satisfying when actualized in the context of meaningful relationship.

Q: I guess you have to fulfill the drives before meaning becomes available.

Ba: It has often been believed (by Humanist psychologists in particular) that drive must be satisfied before draw can be met. Draw is seen as a potentiality waiting for the right conditions. This is mistaken. Draw draws all the time. It is the recognition of draw that humans engage when there is no fear that drives may go wanting. Draw includes all attributes that contribute to human well-being such as aesthetics (beauty), knowledge (intimacy), freedom (responsibility), and ultimately wholeness, spirituality, and self-knowledge.

Darwin was also drawn to meaning. His entire theory gives meaning to evolution. To develop one of the most potent theories of meaning in recent times and to ignore meaning itself exudes irony. Humans need meaning and Darwin obviously really needed meaning. When evolution is rewritten from the perspective of meaning, self-knowledge will become the centerpiece for all education.

Q: Suggesting that meaning is an engine of evolution fundamentally challenges my meaning of, well, meaning. I cannot accept what you say about meaning without more specific examples.

Ba: Fleeing pain is a drive; awakening well-being and wholeness is the draw. Sex is a drive, intimacy is the draw. Hunger is a drive; harmony is the draw. Darwin highlighted the drives, meaning highlights the draw. When the drives dominate, the draws are malnourished. When the draws dominate, the drives are satisfied. There is no lack.

Q: I followed you until the last statement about lack.

Ba: The plumage of the bird maintains its camouflage value even as its beauty inspires. Survival and meaning co-exist. Nothing is lost by acknowledging the draw. Catastrophic loss—no inspiration, no deeper meaning in life—comes when we adhere to only the drives.

Q: Does meaning bring us closer to self-knowledge?

Ba: The search for meaning is a medium in which self-knowledge can flourish. When there is no search for meaning, there is only conscienceless drive. Driven people can become twisted. Such people attempt to thwart others' search for meaning. It is unbearable to them that others should have what they do not. On a grand scale, twistedness is obvious in the oppression of others. On a smaller scale, each of us is twisted when we have lost our relationship to meaning. Some symptoms of twistedness are lack of enjoyment in another's success (and delight in their failure), imposing upon children and others with lesser capacity, and ignoring or rationalizing the suffering in life.

This poem celebrates that meaning is in our essence:

You are a Philosopher (whether you like it or not)

You are what you mean.
You mean what you are.
It's non-negotiable.

So, friend, be conscious of your intent.
All is relationship.
And you will be well.

Chapter Five:
The Creative Flow of Need

Ba: For a person living self-knowledge, meaning becomes the creative flow of need.

Q: Stop. This is one too many new ideas for me. I'm comfortable with knowledge as beyond reason. Self-observation and self-inquiry confirm your approach to conscience. The understanding of relationship as a place of self-discovery matches my intuition. I've always sensed limitations in the Darwinian Theory. Meaning seems like a fair revision—more inclusive of how I see my humanity. But whatever are you doing when you toss in a notion like "the creative flow of need"?

Ba: I appreciate the challenges that self-knowledge brings. The conditioned confusions and attendant fears have been around so long that deficiency has become the norm. All too often we believe that we are encased in fear, or that something fearful is imminent. We have become addicted to pathology, continually asking: "what's wrong," and "what's abnormal?" The pain of leaving the familiar seems unbearable. We even doubt our own capacity to grow, to appreciate new insights.

Q: Some of the attachment to the familiar applies to me, but I also enjoy new learning. Perhaps I can reach for the creative flow of need if you tell me why it is necessary.

Ba: I am describing life as it is, life as it is lived with self-knowledge. Need is not a burdensome notion. It is not an obligation. Need refers to that which will bring forth well-being. Meaning transforms into participation in the creative flow of need for a person living self-knowledge.

Q: Well-being for whom? For all the people involved? For life? What field are you talking about?

Ba: Well-being maximizes the strengths of everyone involved in a given situation. At the same time well-being minimizes unnecessary suffering. Well-being does not imply perfection.

Q: You're using it in an evolutionary sense. You simply mean well-being is the best adaptation to circumstances.

Ba: Thank you. Well-being is implicit in the creative flow of need. Personally, by inquiring into meaning I have come to participate in self-knowledge. And so I found my wife.

Q: Run that by me again.

Ba: My wife continually challenged my assumptions, my conditionings. When those challenges brought forth emotional intensity, including rage and anger, she did not back away. We struggled but always returned to self-inquiry, self-observation, and meaning. Participation in the creative flow of need emerged. We co-evolved in the matrix of conscientious relationship, of mutual well-being.

Q: What do you mean by the term "creative flow"?

Ba: Life is endlessly creating and recreating itself. Each of us is unique. New capacities appear in species continually. This stream of life is the flow. The creativity should be obvious as, at the moment, one of its supreme creations is the two bi-peds using their mysterious brain and engaging this dialogue.

Q: I will try to put it all together. Creation flows in an endless stream of new forms and new capacities. Those capacities appear in response to need. They are not random. But what has that to do with each of us, as individuals?

Ba: We'll get to that in shortly. I am a bit surprised that you didn't object to my disavowal of randomness as a key driver for evolution. Random mutation and subsequent selection are canon to the physical evolutionists that you referred to earlier.

Q: I did have random mutation in mind as well. If I understood how this creative flow of need lives in me, or at least is important to me, then I thought the randomness issue might lose importance.

Ba: Fair enough. I find your approach in seeing how the creative flow of need lives in us as individuals insightful. We are a microcosm of the Universe. If it's true, if it's knowledge, then it lives as each of us, hence the potency of self-knowledge.

The creative flow of need arises effortlessly, spontaneously, and inexorably. The capacity to participate in it is innate; the capability to do so is a quality of self-knowledge. Creativity is the expression of need. The creative flow of need has no beginning and no end—an eternal fount that is always new, refreshing, and surprising. It is always a discovery, or perhaps an uncovering or a revelation of the simple, sane, and obvious, though often not easy to live.

Q: If it is sane and obvious, if it's an evolutionary draw to well-being, than why isn't it easy to live?

Ba: Participating as the creative flow of need is the operating mode of self-knowledge. Unnecessary fears block the flow. Self-absorptions block the flow. Attachment to family and cultural narratives blocks the flow. Previous needs called forth our species but required that fears and attachments to the drives predominate. Now, need has changed, as it always will, and so new creativity emerges from the flow.

Q: Can you describe this creative flow specifically?

Ba: Participation in the creative flow of need is an ontological event; it is only about being. Becoming arises out of being effortlessly. Doing is implicit and explicit in self-knowledge due to the continuous participation in the creative flow of need. There is no separation between being and becoming; no separation between need and response. The creative flow of need emerges again and again and again…Therefore it cannot be fully described. Each situation calls forth a new expression. Yet it is possible to perceive qualities of the creative flow of need.

This poem suggests a bit about the creative flow of need:

Dynamics

I have healed a few people with my hands
Others with my words; many more with my presence.
I have read the thoughts of others
And flown directly into the progenitor of our sun.

Mind precedes body
Consciousness precedes mind
Self precedes consciousness.

The only value of diet and exercise
is to know the mind.
The only value of psychology
is to know consciousness.
The only value of spiritual work
is to inquire into the Self.

> The right question is more important than
> the answer.

Q: I am beginning to understand what you mean by the creative flow of need. But you have not linked it to me. And you must; otherwise, it remains a cosmological insight that I have no way to apply.

Ba: How about the relationship between the creative flow of need and compassion?

Q: That would probably do it.

Ba: The following inquiry into compassion reveals rich qualities of the creative flow of need.

Compassion

Ba: Compassion arises as participation in the creative flow of need. Compassion requires no effort. While participating in compassion, the perception of need is of the same breath as the response to it. This action moment may last a nano-second or scores of years. In either case it simply is what is, and untouchable by rationalization or concern for traditional comforts.

Compassion has nothing to do with recognition from others. Often it cannot even be recognized by others. Often it is vilified by others. While enduring the hardships imposed by the ignorance of others, unpleasant and unwelcome as it may be, there is no doubting the compassion itself. Nor is there loss of freedom, no matter how severe the impositions.

Q: That reminds me of the lives of saints and sages. They were responding to their perceptions of the needs of the moment without care for what others thought or the hardships imposed.

Ba: Yes, they often used religion as a vehicle for it provided them the greatest leeway.

However, compassion is always and everywhere a quality of self-knowledge. Religion was abandoned if it did not serve compassion, as indicated by their biographies and the histories of their times.

Q: If compassion requires sundering from religion at times, it must not abide by other social norms either.

Ba: Compassion does not need history; nor does compassion need conventional notions of "fair." Compassionate people do not compare their actions with another's. Their actions, indeed their life, arise from the creative flow of need, not a measurement of what a person has, does, or has done. Likewise, compassion pays no attention to socially constructed notions such as providing for the underprivileged or "underdog."

Q: I cannot comprehend living this way.

Ba: To comprehend is to hold something. How can you hold the creative flow? In thought, comprehension means to understand how ideas are linked together. Therefore, yes, the creative flow of need cannot be comprehended, thus exposing the paucity of comprehension as a way to view self and life.

Q: I meant that living this way sounds difficult, if not impossible.

Ba: Compassion participates in the creative flow of need. This exquisite flow embodies attunement to the emerging reality, to life as it is. That attunement lies beyond thought. How can a spiral nebula hold together? How does the forest maintain itself? What is a human mind/body? What do we know of its nature? Of its origination? Mystery upon mystery.

Equally mysterious, the person living self-knowledge does not have "reasons" for a compassionate action. It does not generate in reason. It generates in knowledge. Those who use reason to assess the action will often find it difficult.

Q: So you are not engaging this dialogue to teach?

Ba: Not to teach, not to save anyone, not to make money. Neither these nor similar motivations influence my activity. This is what is needed. I have no notion of what the outcomes will be.

Q: How do you earn your livelihood? Is it possible to live self-knowledge, to be in the creative flow of need and therefore be compassionate and work at a job?

Ba: Self-knowledge awakens us to our vocation. A vocation is a calling from the draw, an insight into the activity that is meaningful and productive. It calls to each of us differently, for our unique blend of talents is a creative expression of need.

Q. Will you name your vocation?

Ba: Don't get me started for I will go on for hours. Colleagues call me passionate about my work. It's just the expression of my vocation.

Q: I would like to know.

Ba: I can only offer a poem.

This poem connects meaning, the creative flow of need, and vocation:

Prophecy

I have a well-established and justly deserved
reputation
As a Prophet
On all matters of interpersonal relationships

Especially in family, with children and in partnerships.
I gain my income in this way.
Hiding behind such terms as consultant, coach, counselor and teacher.

There is an old Persian story.
A man comes rushing up to the market square in frenzy because he has lost his camel.
"Has anyone see my camel?" he cries.
Three blind men are standing nearby.
"Is he old?" asks the first.
"Yes, yes. Where did he go?"
"Is he blind in his right eye?" asks the second.
"Yes, yes. Tell me where he is!"
"Is his left rear foot lame?" asks the third.
"'Yes, yes, yes. Now where did he go?"
The camel owner is desperate.
"We don't know," all three reply.
The camel owner is nonplussed.
"Then how did you know all about my camel?"
"Well, I caught his scent by the bush," replies the first, "and went over there and found a tuft of his coat. It was dry and crumbly and so the camel must have been old."
The second blind man speaks. "I joined my friend and ran my hand along the bush. Only the left side of the leaves was eaten so he must have been blind in the right eye."

"And so I felt along the ground and found uneven indentations," says the third. "Only a lame camel would make those tracks."
That's how easy prophecy is.
The camel owner only has to learn to look.
The signs are everywhere.
I would have thought he could do it on his own.
It was his camel!

Here's my prophecy.
It will not be diplomacy
Or war
Or computer simulation modeling
Or democracy
Or socialism
That will end the confusion, hurt, and pain
That characterizes our era.

Nor will it be
Poetry
Art
Dance
Music
Meditation
Shamanic journeys
Or any human artifact.
Faith in any of the above is vanity.
Denial of the pain
Behind the masks of allegiance and desire.

Chapter Five: The Creative Flow of Need

The change that is coming will be as radical
As leaving the savannah to inhabit northern niches.
As leaving Australopithecus to become homo sapien.
And perhaps as radical as leaving the water to live on land.
Yes, you did all of these.
The experiences are locked in every cell in your body—
if you only knew how to look.
It is your body.

Perfection ends and is found
In the ceaseless adaptations
Of emotional intelligence.
Of learning to love ourselves
Without allegiance and desire
Without conceptualizing perfection
But by looking back
Way back
To unfabricated primordial beginnings.

What kind of world would that be?
As if color were added to black and white,
flowers to grassland,
meaning beyond metaphor
respect for all life
The end of imposed competitive struggle.
Darwin and Malthus will be seen as icons

Of confusion.
More ridiculous than Newton in an Einsteinian
quantum mechanics world
But necessary for evolution.

Increasing complexity is the dominant evolutionary
dynamic.
Physical, cognitive, emotional.
All three just one.
Wisdom awakening.

Family, extended family, friends, peers
the crucibles of emotional learning.
Religious authority, poisonous pedagogy, ignorance
of the way children organize their world—
cripplers of emotional learning.

In every interaction with children you are choosing.
Don't pretend.
Evolution is in your hands, heart, and mind,
Yes, yours.
You.
Tag, you're it.

What do children really need?
What are their natural developmental imperatives?
Do you know?
Ask:

Can parenting and education be optimal without
this knowledge?
Ask:
Can evolution be optimal with implementation of
this knowledge?
Ask:
Whose children are they?
Not just the ones from your loins.
All of them.
Whose children are they?

Knowing the natural needs of children
Is every clue you need
To know where your species and life is headed.
It's that simple.
Be wise like the blind men,
Not frantic like the camel owner.
This is our world.
Earth—a gift beyond imagining.
Life—and the ability to love.

So here is the prophecy:
When at least 33% of resources are dedicated to
nurturing the natural needs of children
We are one generation from the end of pollution,
pain, war, and hypocrisy.
Let no one say my prophecies do not include deliverables.

Q: I had no idea how personal this really is.

Ba: Self-knowledge, the creative flow of need, and compassion call on you, as you are. This is not about fitting into an abstract spiritual template.

Q: I was just getting used to the impersonality of compassion—the lack of concern with what others think, with how long it takes, or with the outcome. But if we are unique, it follows that our compassionate actions will also be unique. It's as if each of us is an instrument in a symphony.

Ba: I distrust metaphors. They might work well for others, but self-knowledge, to me, lies beyond comparison, no matter how sophisticated. Self-observation and self-inquiry provide an unadorned approach to finding out how self-knowledge and compassion live as me, as you.
You have brought us to the personal. I acknowledge that we need to know one another to deepen our dialogue.

These two poems attempt to express lend insight into compassion:

Place

Annie Smith and her wife spent their lovely and lovers' 1850s life
On a riverboat in the wild Columbia Gorge
Taking photos; partying with amateur photographers.

They knew where they belonged.
Ramana Maharishi, the brilliant sage of the last century,
Awoke, went straight to Arunachala Hill and never left.
Arunachula lived in him, as him.
Shaman Tom Pinkson
Makes love with Mt. Shasta
Great Spirit permeates.

I am different.
Drifting, wandering,
Nowhere home.

Oh, I have lived in and loved the mountains,
And the shore, and the sea.
The jungle and the forest have sheltered me,
Cities have always been my friend.
I have lived in spacious beautiful homes
for long stretches of time;
some built by my own hand.

I have captained large, sustainable building projects,
Led a thousand seminars
And ecstatically embraced Earth.
I have engaged everywhere and everyhow—
Soho loft building with five artistes in the early 70s,

Two-family spiritual retreat in Hawaii throughout
the 80s,
Hip Sierra environmental rural community through-
out the 90s,
Progressive Portland in the 00s.
Guided a 20-member spiritual community
and a 100-person educational organization.
I should be the Woody Guthrie poster child.
But this land is not my land.
This Columbia River rushing in my backyard is not
my river.
I want no part of Whitman or Snyder
And refuse mythically laced community.

Alone, wandering,
Consciousness the only field,
A field of play, not a place.

Yet I love every blade of grass,
How could they not be me?
Every rock implies life;
Every life is the trace of spirit.
The end of the dialectic.
Consciousness is to place
As Spirit is to religion.
Consciousness/Spirit has no opposite.
Mystery upon mystery.
Paradox upon paradox.

No home means no myth.
No myth means no community.
It's like the story about the person who dreams the village well water is poisoned.
Anyone who drinks it will go crazy.
He alerts his community. They don't listen.
They drink the water, he does not.
They go crazy. They think him crazy.
Does he drink the water?
Do you?

You want these connections to make sense?
Question every tradition, every authority, every belief.
No act has any other meaning
than that which you give it.
Ask.
Does that act have meaning?
Does tradition bind?
Do you need it to?
What would it mean if you had no home?
Who would be your community?
Do not confuse alone with loneliness.
I am just i.
The blessings of consciousness.
Ah...

Last Words

Dear Children:

I am so very old
Bones disintegrating to dust,
Memories jumbled pixels,
No resistance to chaos.
This may be my last moment of lucidity.

So please indulge me and listen.

You are not what you do.
Your value is not in your performance.
(I know I have said this before but please indulge
the ramblings of a dying man.)
It does not matter if you are a judge, a minister, an
editor, a guru, an athlete, a teacher, a sanitation
worker, a clerk, a CEO, a poet...
It doesn't matter.
If you believe you are what you do, you are in
prison.
You are looking in the wrong place.
Rumi said it best:
All my life I've been knocking on the door,
Only to find out I was on the inside the whole time.

Chapter Five: The Creative Flow of Need

I know why you do it.
Why you judge yourself continuously by your performance.
You know why too.
They didn't mean it.
They suffered the same abuse.
So did their parents.
How far back do you want to go?
I am that old.
And it goes all the way back.
All the way.
The only question is:
Will you end it?

Know who you are.
The only freedom there is.

I'm fading...

Here's how.
Stop complaining.
Just stop.
Plugging that leak vivifies.

Look at nature deeply.
What is wasted?
What isn't a miracle?
Where can you find an end?

Learn to trust by giving.
Emptiness is the field of surrender.
Helpless, defenseless,
Quantum potential dispersed trans-galactically,
You be.

And that will be that.
Time (the ultimate cosmic joke) capitulates
And all associated fears dissolve.

Oh time, are you coming for me?
How do you know who you are?
Who is your mother, your father?
Where do you live?
I salute you and ignore you simultaneously.
And remind you
That I am older than you,
Friend to your parents,
And have long disowned the things you claim.

Q: Time loses its hold, fear dissolves, and we know who we are.

Ba: In the midst of this mysterious attunement, compassion acts without doubt and without reason. Compassion's matrix is self-knowledge and self-knowledge is attuned to the whole, to the Universe. This self is of the essence, of the patterns, rhythms, and emerging whole. We are a microcosm. Compassion lives as this.

Q: Working for compassion must be a great goal to have.

Ba: Any effort made to be compassionate pushes us further from compassion. Effort is the result of "figuring things out," of creating balance sheets and choosing the supposed best course of action. The ancient problem appears. Who is doing the figuring? For what aim? Most often, people efforting compassion do it "for others," thus revealing their basic alienation and separation.

The same conundrum exists for organized religion. In the business of trying to save the masses by convincing them to adhere to its path, which despite cultural differences are remarkably similar in their use of guilt, fear, and insistence that they are the authority on what happens after death, religion rallies its minions to greater and greater efforts. These include surrendering a disproportionate share of wealth for the institution, trying to do sanctioned good deeds, and supporting political agendas. These confusions are a dazzling neon sign pointing to their thinking that separation is not only the obvious human condition but is ordained to be so. The ordination of separation equals the ordination of religion.

Believing compassion to be dependent upon effort obfuscates the creative flow of need. People become dependent upon extrinsic sources to tell them they are good, the religious institution and its artifacts are venerated, and separation rules.

Q: But if working towards compassion doesn't yield compassion, why are so many attracted to doing just that?

Ba: The power of the draw to compassion compels us to do all we can. Humans do desperately want to actualize the goodness that is their nature. The urge to transcendence draws each of us. We do not have to have the lower drives satisfied in order to respond to the higher. We are always drawn, always responding. It is only the illusion of separation, the ignorance of self-knowledge that leaves us clinging to religions and fruitlessly trying to effort our way to compassion.

Compassion cannot be defined or owned. All claims to standardizing compassion are claims, are attempts at staking a territory, and are the result of thinking that compassion is a commodity, a currency, a thing. There are no compassionate Christians, compassionate Buddhists, compassionate Conservatives; there is only compassion, unadorned, creative, mysterious, and accessible through participation in genuine knowledge.

Perception of need and the simultaneously arising action are the natural expressions of self-knowledge, of being. No learning of extrinsic systems of morality is necessary; more often they get in the way. As it is natural, it is an intrinsic human capacity. All humans are born with the capacity for compassion, with the capacity for self-knowledge, with the capacity to live as human beings.

On Genius and Self-Knowledge

Ba: Appreciating the difference between genius and self-knowledge helps us deepen our connection to the creative flow of need.

Q: The word *genius* refers to some specific capacity that we are born with. But you have said that we are born with the capacity for self-knowledge as well.

Ba: Yes, but go slowly. Genius is inherent and as natural as breathing. Once activated, genius calls forth great and immediate concentration and inventiveness. Original and unique, the results of genius often radically change the "reality" of their given discipline.

Q: Then genius is the same as self-knowledge.

Ba: Not exactly. Genius is the gift of the talents with which we were born. It is expressed in a given discipline such as music or physics, or interpersonal relationships.

Q: Do we have to actualize self-knowledge to express our genius?

Ba: No. Genius comes forth when the conditions in life allow for it. It is a sign of our alienation that relationships with one another, and especially with children, are not centered on awakening genius. The opposite is usually the case:

conditioning children to separation and to achieving politically correct cultural skills inhibits the activation of genius. Rewards and punishments probably do the same. When that happens, as happens to so many, special and rare life circumstances must ensue for genius to express itself. Reliance on special and rare conditions is unnecessary suffering.

Q: What are these conditions that allow for genius?

Ba: No one knows. But as I said, we gravely limit the opportunities for the genius in each of us to come forward by the way we treat children.

Most of us never suspect that we have the capacity for genius. So much unnecessary suffering follows. By ignoring our own genius, we have lost the precious opportunity to treat others in a way that would allow their genius to come forward. When we support one another's genius, we often bask in the delight of geniuses interconnecting.

Q: Genius sounds like a specific instance of the creative flow of need.

Ba: The expression of genius is a breakthrough into the flow of creativity that lends new insight into ourselves and our world. But it is not self-knowledge.

The quality of the being of the person distinguishes genius from self-knowledge. No one with self-knowledge, no matter how intellectually brilliant, could be a Nazi, as was Heidegger. If you consider some of the other well-recognized geniuses, similar conclusions become obvious—they run the gamut from mean-spirited to self-wounding to social fools. Some spiritual geniuses lack self-knowledge. It is not just idiosyncratic; it is that genius is innate and therefore makes no demands on the whole being whereas the capacity for self-knowledge is innate but must be actualized. Self-knowledge requires the whole of our being and nothing less.

Genius does not require any particular relationship to suffering whereas self-knowledge insists on a conscious, unflinching participation in suffering. Self-knowledge does not attempt to solve the conundrums in a particular discipline. Genius is often either self-absorbed or oblivious. Self-knowledge is neither.

Q: I notice that you left "need" out when talking about genius.

Ba: I am not suggesting separation between the expression of genius and the creative flow of need. I am saying, however, that the genius does not know of their momentary participation in the creative flow of need. Their knowledge then becomes information. As such, it rarely awakens self-knowledge in others though it does have the salubrious effect of challenging conditioned belief systems.

Q: Doesn't Mozart inspire you?

Ba: Sure, as does John Lennon and Einstein and Emily Dickenson and Tesla and Froebel and many, many others. I leap with joy when their expressions take hold in me. They have been able to bring their moments of creativity to the rest of us. I have been challenged again and again by their work, and I am grateful with every breath. But that doesn't mean I neglect everyday genius such as nurturing a child properly—not as common as most believe—or that I need to venerate the individual who is expressing genius.

This poem describes an oft-neglected expression of genius.

The Only Skill That Counts

Everything about awakening is upside down and inside out.
Nothing is as it appears to be and yet we all say the same thing:
It's the only reality there is.
Take skill-learning.
The only one that counts is:
Letting go.
Why ?
Here' a taste of what happens.
You participate in
-dedication to children
-reverence as the ground
-intentionality
-intimations of impartiality
-time freedom

-fear morphing into challenge; allegiance into
emotional discernment
-hope dying; commitment ablaze

And indubitably, you see
-dedication to children is the only sure sign of
awakening
- constraint lives only by your fiat
- the inmates are running the asylum

Letting go reveals the natural draw—
A yearning
Personal and impersonal
Inevitable and inexorable
Not pushed by ambition.
Oh, for a culture that sees this,
That lets go of then and when and chooses now,
That lets go of that and chooses this.

Q: But look at the effort geniuses make to bring their insights to the rest of us.

Ba: As they will tell you, they have no choice. They know their vocation. That comes with the insight.

Q: And that moment of insight, that experience in which they touch pure creativity is not sufficient for self-knowledge?

Ba: Amazing, isn't it? But what is an experience? Is any experience sufficient for self-knowledge?

Q: I read all the time about so-called spiritual experiences that bring enlightenment. There are white lights, near-death experiences, spontaneous awakenings, shaman-induced rituals...I could go on and on.

Ba: Then let's look more closely at experiences. They are certainly an aspect of who we are. And non-ordinary experiences do have value in bringing expanded awareness. But do they allow participation in the creative flow of need? Most importantly, does the moment of the experience equate to the actualization of self-knowledge?

Chapter Six:
On Non-Ordinary Experiences

Q: You do see non-ordinary experiences as valuable?

Ba: I do. I have had such experiences.

Q: What were they?

Ba: Here's an autobiographical poem that references a couple of them.

A poem describing non-ordinary experiences:

Early Journeys

Many have asked me to write of my life's journey.
It doesn't turn me on.
Each of us must find ourselves
Self-knowledge has no form.
What good would another story be?
Too many emulate.
The Buddha never followed the Eight Fold Path.
Krishnmurti got zapped under a tree
Despite all his talk about insight.

Chapter Six: On Non-Ordinary Experiences

And on and on.
You will never do what I did.
How could you?

There's an old Irish story.
A neighbor comes rushing to a friend's house.
"They've chosen the lottery winners!"
"What's that to me?"
"You've won!"
"What's that to you?"

Don't be fooled.
So what if I lived inner lights?
Relived my birth?
Hooked a ride on the DNA spiral
Through countless eons of evolutionary history?
Can you fill up on my emptiness?

Caveat delivered.

I've spoken these thoughts to others
they still want the autobio.
I told them my dislike of mythologizing life.
They said inspiration can be found in the lives of others.
Which is true.
So here I go.

Something happened at 32
Makes the story worth telling.

Cascading nectar drenched my being
While I sat quietly
Beyond bliss
Beyond sorrow
Beyond breath
Beyond Life
Beyond Death

Pure Awareness

Did anything before it presage its arrival?
Had it been heralded?

Ancestry?
There were Rabbis in the Old Country
But my parents were modern.
Middle-class American household
With love, rage, confusion, success, and failure.
A tortured childhood with many moments of happiness.
Nothing special.

An event at 17 mattered.
A friend driving us home at 2 in the morning
Smashed into a barrier going 40.
Before seatbelts and crumple zones.

(Thanks, Detroit)
Through the windshield.
And into outer space
Travelling at warp speeds
In endless black radiance
Soft liquid velvet
Fear-free
Two lights in the far far distance
Approaching at fantastic speed
(These movement words confound)
Very close
Very bright
Cocooned in energy
High-speed transmission
With only one verbal message:
"This knowledge will be available as you need it."
Then a question:
"Do you want to go back?"
My answer:
"You decide."
(They did seem to have a greater perspective.)

Sirens.
On a stretcher.
I started to rise,
Knew I wasn't hurt.
"Hey," from the EMT, "lie down!
Your neck was on jagged glass
And you've been unconscious.

(Well, not exactly but I couldn't tell him that.)
You're going to the hospital."
Whatever.

At the moment before the accident I was 50
pounds overweight
Bitingly bled all 10 fingernails
Believed no girl would want me.
Self-abused in a thousand ways;
Some of which I believed pleasurable.
Hating stupidity, hating myself.

Well this round trip to somewhere
at an unknowable speed
the only sights liquid black
and pinpoints turning to fields of liquid gold
does something to anyone.

And here's what it did to me:
Exponential expansion of trust, of freedom
Calmly exhilarated beyond questioning
Illogically confident
Certain that self-knowledge is essential and not
what anyone thinks it is
(How can it be when thought is but a fraction of its
field?)

Blasted onto the bottom rung of the ladder,
Tilted by the demon of honesty

as I lived my confusion
in extraordinary bouts of hope and fear.
Romantic love knocked me on my ass.
Realizing as I write
that my endless capacity for love was at play
but projected on the object of my desire.
So that had to end.
Poetically, by the suburban pseudo-hip overdose
death of my sister.

Conscious suffering,
Even while my personas flailed
And balked and led me on.

Sentimentality shattered; lost but lighter in fear.
Stumbling around America.
Have you ever been so fucking tired that you cannot listen to another word?
I have no idea why so many people were so good to me.
Strong women giving succor in sweet silent embrace.
A philosopher carpenter giving patient shelter, pointing in as the way.
And Great Nature, stunningly beautiful, ruthless—
the Badlands scoured, the desert emptied, the ocean destroyed limitations.
How could I be so alone, so hurt, so angry—
And then so devastated

when Love descended out of nowhere, for no reason,
and the waterfall of tears turned the ground into a swamp, a sinking morass—
quicksand with no definition, no markers, no direction, no dimension.

Twenty days passed.
In the middle of the twenty-first night I awoke in a trance.
Dug a shallow grave.
Machete'd bamboo into sticks,
Arranged the sticks as a body,
And laid the effigy of myself to rest.
Buried, entombed, immobile,
Acknowledged and cast off.
Then, scalding grief.

Three days later the trance lifted.
Ablutions in a puka fed by an untainted mountain stream.
Shining red berries on wild coffee bushes,
Ambrosia masquerading as passion fruit
The mosquitoes a chorus of the heavenly hum.

My trek continued miles north to the Waimanu Valley.
Inland I turned, away from the ocean,

So tender its roaring immensity threatened annihilation.

In I went, senses suffused in the sweet scent of decay,
sharp azure sky switching figure and ground with tall verdant foliage
so that at times I seemed to be walking upside down.
The first home of Kamehameha appeared, a disappearing ruin of mossy brown rocks.
The ground littered with hard round kokui nuts.
I set up my tent, ate my pumpkin seeds, and went to sleep.

Further inland, to Hawaii's tallest waterfall.
Bathing in the cold pool at the bottom.
Looking up, following the glistening descent of a single drop,
Falling free, only to rejoin the other drops in the water below.
Time to leave.

Postscript: Last night I heard you say:
Give us more.
Give your word perfection standard a rest!
We'll decide for ourselves.

Okay, I will.

> But not right now.
> But I have one question:
> How did you get in my head?
> And one caveat:
> Now that you're there, be gentle!

Q: I will be gentle. Tell me what you find valuable in experiences such as these.

Ba: Non-ordinary experiences are the necessary antidote to fear, loneliness, alienation, and many of the attendant pathologies of separation. Non-ordinary experiences are so important, and so feared by those who believe in separation, that those who have them are either glorified, placed in an institution (mental or religious), vilified, or completely discounted. If non-ordinary experiences were brought out of the closet, feminism and gender liberation would be revealed as mini-ripples in the fabric of a changing society.

Q: Are you claiming that people who have non-ordinary experiences are necessarily wise or socially just?

Ba: No and yes. No, not by virtue of the experience itself, though there is a strong chance that social injustice becomes an anathema. Yes, in that if there were cultural support for non-ordinary experiences, then respect for one another would become the norm and social justice an unremarkable lived fact. We would know that human consciousness has extraordinary capacities. Then, each of us, having touched these capacities in ourselves, would realize that others carry the same gift that we do. That engenders respect. And respect for one another brings social justice.

Q: But society does not have the right regard for non-ordinary experience?

Ba: It is the discounting of them that is ludicrous. Every society has detailed recorded accounts of non-ordinary experiences. The mandalas found in such diverse places as Hopi sand painting, gothic cathedrals, Himalayan monasteries, and South American pottery attempt to capture some of the visual phenomenology of one type of non-ordinary experience. Poetry and spiritual philosophy remind people that non-ordinary experiences exist as well as attempt to record the qualities of some of the experiences. Certain expressions of music and movement do this as well. In fact, when we admit that non-ordinary experiences are real, the signs are everywhere.

Q: What about spirituality? There, our culture does approve of such experiences.

Ba: Only for saints and sages, and then in a religious context. Non-ordinary experiences inform all spiritual inquiries. Where would any religion be without "miracles?" Only the promise of non-ordinary experiences—either in life or the "hereafter"—can inspire the use of the time, money, and consuming efforts that most spiritual paths require.

Indeed, how can spiritual leaders claim to know anything about the supposed afterlife unless they have "seen" it during non-ordinary experiences? How can spiritual leaders claim to be ordained by an "unseen" God or by colleagues in their lineage unless they were privy to non-ordinary experiences? In these ways non-ordinary experiences engender faith. Everyone attending any form of religious worship affirms the actuality of non-ordinary experiences.

Denying non-ordinary experiences reeks of hypocrisy. No, wait, the pinnacle of hypocrisy reserves such experiences for the saints and sages recognized by the religion.

Q: That means that non-ordinary experiences are inherent, a natural human capacity.

Ba: Yes, and the capacity implies the faculty to know their value and meaning. These experiences only seem non-ordinary from the separation perspective. Given the proper education and opportunity that which is now called *non-ordinary* would be known as a quality of the human mind. Consequently, there would be considerably less fear and loneliness; the confusion of separation would begin to disappear.

Preparation and Reentry

Ba: In the highly sensitive and vulnerable moment of non-ordinary experiences and their immediate aftermath, the individual can easily be impressed with the "rightness' of almost anything. Ordinary reality constructs have been blown apart. Established crap detectors developed through years of social learning (in an often threatening world) are no longer in place. A risk, a surrender has occurred and impressionability rivals that of the newborn.

Q: I guess that's why psychedelics have had such varied effects.

Ba: Non-ordinary experiences temporarily blow away conditioning. In order to prevent the imprinting of culturally accepted thoughts, icons, and practices—in other words, in order to not simply switch one conditioning for another, or worse, to "re-up" on the former conditioning—non-ordinary experiences are best accessed in nature or in clean, unadorned spaces. It is the mark of a spiritual mentor to choose the place that allows the greatest freedom, inquiry, and lack of stress, and to eliminate reminders of previous conditioning.

In most cases psychedelics were consumed without guidance and without regard to the individual's moment—whether they were in the throes of an emotionally challenging situation, for example—or the environment they were in. Who they were with and where they were have a powerful effect on their experiences. We should expect wildly varying results.

Q: What is the best moral and psychological support?

Ba: Inundate a person in these moments with a doctrine and there is strong probability that the doctrine will be believed. Therefore, only a non-authoritative, inquiring, and well-informed "re-entry" allows the person to arrive at the meaning of their experience. *Non-authoritative* means that the mentor and support system do not attempt to persuade the person to interpret the non-ordinary experience according to a particular belief system. *Inquiring* means that there is open investigation into the experience and its meaning while no aspect of the experience is pre-judged. *Well informed* means that they have some intimacy with the person and also with spiritual philosophy, transpersonal psychology, and the strengths and weaknesses of the particular mode (or "path") by which the person came to the non-ordinary experience.

Q: That requires a special person.

Ba: Special in our world due to our neglect. A mentor can develop the necessary attributes easily in a society that honors non-ordinary experience.

Q: Must this support be intact for non-ordinary experiences to be valuable?

Ba: Non-ordinary experiences have tremendous power. It would be pretentious to assert that only under the above conditions can their value be actualized. However, the above conditions increase the odds dramatically. Without them, chances for genuine learning are greatly curtailed.

Persecution

Q: Why, then, the persecution of those who contact non-ordinary experiences?

Ba: Non-ordinary experiences subvert. They reveal the fraud and deceit that permeates so much of society's fabric. They reveal the fraud and deceit in our own character. The 1960s were fueled by a relatively large number of people having non-ordinary experiences. Even without proper preparation and re-entry, their subversive power boomed around the world.

At present, religion has cornered the market on non-ordinary experiences. Religionists control preparation and re-entry. Non-ordinary experiences become their property—with all the territoriality and defensiveness that comes with it. If a member of a religion has non-ordinary experiences that lead to contradiction of the doctrine, then that person is marginalized (and often attacked) as an outsider, and perhaps even worse.

Q: Why would religion act this way? Why wouldn't they want all of us to have these experiences? Wouldn't that lead more of us to religious practice?

Ba: Most people turn to religion for compensation of their feelings of separation, loneliness, alienation, despair, and suffering. They are interested in relief and they find it in the structure of the religious institution. Religion thrives as a shelter and a refuge; order and continuity provide its foundation. Disruption becomes sacrilege and a personal affront. Moreover, those in the prison of separation rarely wish for another's liberation unless that liberation has religious sanction and results in religiously approved service.

For all of these reasons, religion resists free access to non-ordinary experiences.

Q: These days many don't follow religion's lead on social issues and personal expression. Why isn't there more interest in non-ordinary experience?

Ba: Most people do not care. What's a small group of heretics or radicals to them? They have their life to lead, their family to take care of. They receive information through the media, which has little interest in non-ordinary experiences. They attend schools and jobs that are designed to further established social agendas. Most people are convinced that their happiness lies outside of self. Suffering defeats them and so they consign the response to religion or therapy. Many simply absorb suffering and reach for the next pleasurable event.

Our colleges and universities share in the apathy. They teach about non-ordinary experiences but do not support direct contact with them.

Maps

Q: What are the differences among non-ordinary experiences?

Ba: There are several categories, or types, or realms of non-ordinary experiences and within these categories, there are infinite variations. Explorers from every time and culture have attempted to map these realms. The map usually reflects the cultures in which the explorer lived. Distilled to their essence, however, their maps share remarkable similarity. To me, this proves that non-ordinary experiences live in every human, that they are as "real" as any other experience. The maps remind us of the presence of non-ordinary experiences—of their power and grace. They awaken intuitive and reasonable appreciation of our rich human endowment. Maps help reveal sacredness. Many of these maps inform religions, or at least elucidate the arcane philosophies of their esoteric practitioners.

Q: For example?

Ba: Every religion has an esoteric center. Those of us who need to contact it will do so. We will find a map and, if we care to, we will find the similarities with other maps.

Q: Have you nothing specific to offer? It feels a bit ethereal at the moment.

Ba: I have written prayer poems to describe the various realms. These writings are not personal reflections. They intend some objectivity, as all maps should. Here's a sampling. Each of the following describes a different realm.

Prayer poems describing non-ordinary realms:

Devotion

Let the center be devotion.
For it is by offering Love
That we are emptied,
And by surrendering all
That Truth can be Known.

The Silent Sound

Silence
Sound
Silence
Sound
Sound of Silence
Silence of Sound
Deep quiet
Peace.

Listen
Can you hear it?
The voice of Emptiness
The Silent Sound of God.

Surrender Your I's

Surrender your I's --
Quietly
Breathing...
Let the balanced peaceful rhythms of the Somatic galaxy
Coalesce into this moment of rapture.
Surrender your I's --
Tranquilly
Breathing... Be the calm focused witness
As subtle somatic current
Rises up...
Unifying body, compassion, and wisdom.
Expand...
Into luminous patterns of electro-magnetic energy...
Ecstasy...
And Beyond...
Liberation...
Breathing...
Silently...
Surrender.
Breathing...
Breathing...
Radiate golden light throughout creation.

Molten Gold

Molten Gold
Floating through the inner galaxy.
Solar spaciousness.
Electric fire-blood.
Flowing... Flowing...
Beyond pulse...
Streaming down luminous golden rivers of radiant purity.
Spiritual transmutation
One with all humanity.
Rising... Rising...
Beyond joy... Beyond sorrow...
Merging into the unity of eternal compassion.
Sunlight Irradiation
Heart opening
One
Flowing... Rising...
Beyond gravity...
Surrender...to...
The silent peace of universal absolution.
Tranquil bliss
Molten Gold.

Chapter Six: On Non-Ordinary Experiences

The Preserver

There is in the Universe
A Preserver.
One who serves continually
As the calm centered balance-point
Around which the eternal dance
Of creation and destruction spiral.
One who illuminates
Through stillness
And lives as the silent witness
At the heart of the Mystery.
Beyond pattern...
Beyond color...
Beyond form...
Beyond life...
Beyond death...
The preserver of all...

O Blessed Spirit of Peace
Taking refuge in the sanctity
And Glory of your luminous Being,
We offer our surrender and acceptance.

The Preserver.

Sacred Ground

Sacred Ground
Source of Universe.
Dimensionless...
No advance, no retreat.
Neither sound nor movement.
Beginningless... Endless...
Seamless... Unlimited... Unmanifest...
Utter Stillness
Sacred Ground.

Q: And you say there is constancy across maps beyond the cultural idiosyncrasies.

Ba: There is. However, the map is not the territory and we should never confuse the two. Intellectually comprehending and explaining the map does not help destroy separation and loneliness. Only traversing the territory does. Nevertheless, for most of us, maps pave the way. They tell us that these territories exist, that we can travel in them, and that there are recognizable signposts. They describe what we need to do to prepare to enter and enjoy the territory and tell us of some of the pitfalls we might encounter.

One caveat: it is important to compare many maps for their descriptions *are* culturally circumscribed. Unless we compare, it is easy to fall into believing that there is one true description.

Q: Are these maps just like road maps? Do they show a territory, with its topography and roads?

Ba: Some do, like the Kabala Tree of Life. However, many maps are encoded in myths and stories. Different characters portray different realms. Their actions then portray the ethics of a person who has experienced that realm. For example, in the sacred Hindu myth, *The Ramayana*, the demon King has had a moment with Brahma, the highest realm of experience. Consequently, he can laugh at Time, for it has no hold on him. He cannot escape expressing his demon nature, however. That he made the intense surrender required to touch Brahma allows him to organize his life to return to Brahma. There is no simple good versus bad but complex weavings of fate and actions compelled by the non-ordinary experience.

Also, non-ordinary experiences have so many variations and often appear in ways uniquely appropriate to the individual so that the "signposts" do not have the uniformity of street signs. If we accept the many shades of paradoxes in the following statement, it is fair to say: *non-ordinary experiences allow universal self-discovery for each individual.*

Experience

Q: If non-ordinary experiences allow self-discovery, why do you differentiate them from self-knowledge?

Ba: Ultimately, non-ordinary experiences are experiences. They have duration, a time span, a beginning and an end. Their unique value is that they expand all previous notions of what it is to be human. They lend multiple perspectives that show the humor of attaching to any one of them and foster humility when we begin to think we have the "right" answer. Done well, with the proper preparation and re-entry, they destroy conceptions of limitation, of certainty, of self-righteousness. They leave us questioning, wondering, curious, clarified, and engaged.

But they do end. Their value is the enrichment they awaken in our being. At some point, we realize that it is being itself that is the clarity, the knowledge, the repository and generator of all experiences. At that moment, attachment to non-ordinary experiences drops away. We know that no experience is inherently more sacred than any other. We know that the totality of being is beingness, is essence, is our very self. Separation falls away. As the "snake" is known to be a rope when seen in the light of day, so separation is known to be an illusion perpetrated through ignorance.

Experience of any type is the sacred fodder by which we come to know ourselves. With this realization, overvaluing experience ceases. The mysterious interweave of experiences played out through the eons is revealed as the field in which we come to know ourselves.

Q: Many who have had non-ordinary experiences speak of them as if they include enlightenment. And they certainly would insist that enlightenment is the same as, or includes, self-knowledge. I have a hard time seeing the differences.

Ba: Those awed and enthralled with non-ordinary experience often, in their humility, see them as proof of God. God is named in many ways including Great Spirit, Vishnu/Shiva, God the Father and the Trinity, Great Nature, and so on. As these experiences can yield special powers (such as healing, paranormal psychological phenomena, super-strength, extreme endurance, and the like), the source of these powers is transferred to the Higher Power. Remarks such as "It [the special power] was given and then taken away," or "it is God or Tara working through me" ring of authenticity to the person and to those awed by the non-ordinary experience and its attendant special power. The spectacular display of non-ordinary experiences cloaks the subtle separation, the mythic claim of being God's conduit. This display is fool's gold. Surrender is surrender; clarity and wisdom are never dazzled.

Q: It seems like too much to ask. Surrender non-ordinary experiences as transient? Given the power of these experiences, I don't see how this can be done.

Ba: Self-inquiry. Inquiring into a non-ordinary experience has given me great courage and perseverance at some of the more challenging moments of my life.

A poem telling of a non-ordinary experience and indicative of self inquiry:

Eagle Talk

High in the mountains in the high desert of Taos
Meditating...
Empty...
Beyond body...
Drifting back...
Vision filled with dancing rainbow mandalas
Visitation in the stratosphere
An eagle.
And I saw the subtleties of the myriad reds and browns of its wings,
And the soft iridescent ivory of its throat and wingtips,
And its wild pungent scent thrilled.

And it spoke to me in Eagle talk.

Our heads within an inch of each other's,
Spinning through endless molecules of space, time, and form.
Galaxies borning and dying
Scintillating fire flying in sharp spikes from the belly of stars
Neverending stream of
Eagle talk eagle talk eagle talk eagle talk eagle talk.

Then, sudden descent.
Plummeting, pulverized by the sudden rocketing into
Vast oceans of shit-colored viscous mud.
Urine and fear sweat frosted on my skin
Every violent thought I'd ever had projectile-vomited through my mind
Engulfed in evil
Yet through it all I heard
Eagle talk eagle talk eagle talk eagle talk eagle talk.

Mountain ranges appeared,
Distinct, brilliant in their simple clarity.
Over we went.
The eagle soared ahead.
Leaving me on the far side of the range.

The next day I was in the post office with the friend at whose house I was staying. I had not mentioned any detail about my experience. He pointed to
A very old man
Whose face would make the wrinkle hall of fame
And said that he was the head of the Native American Church and would I like to meet him and I said sure even though I am shy and nervous about this sort of thing and right after I named my name I blurted
What did the eagle say to me?

He peered at me till my self-consciousness
dropped.
Nodded
Said he would come to my friend's house later.

My friend was an artist who had a house with 16-
foot walls and windows everywhere. Stars shone
blue-white, scintillating and ethereal, in the frigid
night when he walked in
Bent over, ancient
With a paper in his hand.
Before he spoke, I knew what he was going to say.
It was not a memory.
The knowledge simply emerged,
Catalyzed by his being.
It was: you will know what you need to do when
you need to do it.
This was the second time in my life for this kind of
thing.
He knew that.
That's the way it is.
My friend knew nothing of this.
The old man read from his paper:
"Ethical maturity is needed to actualize the vision."
And then he became a young man.
He leaped and danced, going high on the walls
And stood on one hand
And much more.
I know what you are going to say,

Miracles, and secretly wishing for something like
this to happen to you.
Awakening magical consciousness—a homecoming.
But in the context it was ordinary, natural,
As it would be for anyone who had swum in the
evolutionary river
Of the transformation of all forms.
This is who we are
when we are not epistemologically constipated.

We enjoyed tea.
Conversationally, he offered me a warning.
"You have a difficult vision,
A task that will not be readily appreciated.
You must be careful.
At times the vision will seem a speck in the great
distance.
There will be reception and rudeness,
Recognition and desolation,
Wealth and confusion.
Some of this will be caused by you,
And some by others.
Learning which is which
Is one of the gifts of the vision.
The vision is always pure.
Do not fall into the treachery of despair.
You must follow the eagle.
Our hearts beat together on this."

> Then he shook his rattle over me.
> I felt the presence of the Eagle.
> Gentle warmth descended.
> I closed my eyes.
> And he was gone.

Q: I don't see the self-inquiry in the poem.

Ba: The turning to the shaman is, in itself, a form of self-inquiry. I placed myself in relationship with one who would stimulate reflection and inquiry. Notice that he did not interpret my experience. Rather, he invited me to participate in how the vision would play out in my life over time and he reminded me that I had a choice in how to use the power bestowed upon me.

Q: It would be easy to claim divine ordination.

Ba: And there have been times I have been tempted. I attribute the self-inquiry of that time and subsequently to helping me avoid that seductive trap.

Q: I know it sounds odd but self-knowledge is so naked.

Ba: Bare and pure. A person living self-knowledge has no need for any other explanation for existence than existence itself. Each breath is a miracle, each body, from microbe to galaxy, of exquisite design and integrity. What need of the non-ordinary when this resplendent generosity is our very nature?

Q: And how does this relate to the creative flow of need?

Ba: No matter how subtle, in non-ordinary experiences the individual is separate from the experience. In self-knowledge there is simultaneously no separation and the entire multitude exists without censor or modifier. Each form in the multitude is unique, distinct, gloriously bounded yet unity itself, an expression of the creative flow of need and—as are all expressions of the creative flow of need—ready and able to transform into exactly what the conditions require.

This reveals form to be unalterably formless. Form, the unique ever-changing manifestation of need, spontaneously springs from the formless, from the creative flow of need.

Chapter Seven: Ethics

Ba: We have to turn to ethics.

Q: Why?

Ba: Ethics are an extension and expression of consciousness. They exist in each of us, as us. Ethics reveal our emotional and intellectual development, our way of organizing the world. We breathe the life into ethics. To view ethics as standing outside of ourselves implies self-denial. To view ethics as external is an ethic in itself, and one that almost invariably leads to unnecessary suffering.

Q: Compassion is obviously the ethics of living self-knowledge. Why bother with anything else?

Ba: Self-inquiry reveals three aspects of self. We forget that at our peril. Appreciating the ethics of each aspect helps us stay in touch with who we are, not who we wish to be.

Mechanical Ethics

Ba: Mechanical ethics infect everyone. Mechanical ethics arise from conditioning and play out in patterns that seem universal. Mechanical ethics are the ethics of Me.

Q: You used the word "infect" and so imply pathology. But you said that Me is necessary, even vital.

Ba: I did, but under the auspices of I and i. Without reflection and inquiry, Me dominates. We suffer.

Q: Be specific.

Ba: Here are the dynamics of mechanical ethics. First comes the exhortation that we must apply ourselves with strong effort and discipline to be successful. Parents, schools, religions, and governments convince the child that they can do better, that there is always another goal to attain, another record to break, another glory to be had, another improvement to society that must be found. In mechanical ethics, helplessness is bad; failure is acceptable only if you learn from it so there won't be future failures. Outside experts appear to prod us onwards and upwards.

Q: You are referring to the pressure to succeed. Obviously, you think it creates problems.

Ba: Often, the psyche does not easily comply with mechanical ethics. Our individual talents and proclivities often do not match its imposed agendas. Some agendas may make sense, others do not. Boundaries must be imposed, often by force, punishment, and bribery. Anything is justified because the end "cultural success" justifies the means.

Q: I agree. More and more, our culture pushes our children, and everyone, to progress and progress and progress. Now there is a buzz to push our children to lead the global marketplace.

Ba: Not just in our culture. In many Eastern countries, 9-year-olds boys are sentenced to become monks by their parents. They are often isolated and in some instances beaten in order to force them to learn to sit and meditate. The parents of 9-year-old children in the West, who have decided that their kids will be athletes or musicians or superior academic achievers, often withhold affection and approval unless their children accede. When they do agree, abundant rewards follow.

Q: And if they don't, they're seen as rebellious or sick or enemies.

Ba: You seem to have strong feelings about this.

Q: Yes, I'm hurt and angry from constantly being imposed upon.

Ba: Mechanical ethics enforces a new condition: allegiance. We must adhere to the agenda for team, country, religion, and clan. Tradition must be upheld. The work of teammates cannot be negated by our indolence or neglect. The team will lose, the country will be perceived as weak, the religion will be disgraced. Allegiance is reinforced by uniforms, team colors, slogans, and sermons, and by publicizing the supposed catastrophes if the group does not succeed.

Q: It's addicting. When you are young, you can't see any way out of this. It becomes the way to belong. Without some allegiances, there is no membership. Such loneliness becomes unbearable.

Ba: This powerful narcotic prompts young people to die for their country. The families of the deceased are exhorted to believe that their child's death brings them honor. Mechanical ethics suggests that ignoring injury in an athletic contest is more important than failing the team. Quitting equals sin. Superstition and taboo reinforce adherence.

Q: But if you don't quit, if you make the required sacrifices, then you are a hero.

Ba: Allegiance needs heroes. Tradition needs heroes. If a team member falters, the legacy of the hero is brought to bear. Athletic teams retire numbers, build monuments, and establish halls of fame. Religions trace lineages, build monuments, and glorify martyrs. Countries distort and extol their histories, construct museums, celebrate founders.

Clans deify ancestors. When everyone buys into the tradition, then the tradition dictates the ethics. That tradition then validates the parent, teacher, and priest as the arbiter of right and wrong.

Q: Do I hear the wrong use of conscience in this? Of course I do.

Ba: Let's specify how it occurs. In a vain attempt to be consistent, the institution must develop an abstract notion of virtues and define the virtuous person. Thus, a devout Catholic woman does not use birth control and disapproves of others who do. Birth control cannot be virtuous no matter the circumstances.

Even more abstractly, abstruse philosophies of virtue validated by academicians allow nations to justify telling citizens how they should behave. This "should" has nothing to do with the way people act, nor with their core natures, nor with the social pressures they feel. A clear example is Germany's version of allegiance to Nietzsche's superman and Wagner's stereotypes and many of the citizens' subsequent willingness to embrace Nazism. Abstract virtues mean nothing except for their propaganda value in holding a population in prison.

Mechanical ethics, replete with tradition and reinforced by allegiance, are the inevitable result of a consciousness mired in separation. Distorted and perverted expressions of conscience must follow.

Here's a poem about Me claiming ethical insight:

Smarmy Shock-Jock with Homophobic Undertones

Sports shock jock finishes reciting statistics to support his view that athletes who challenge conventional social norms *on the average* (emphasis his) perform poorly when compared to their potential as rated by scouts and managers *who should know* (emphasis his) and

then he tells of his dear old dad
and how his dad punished him if he went near a joint
or hinted at sex in high school.
And how the punishment would get physical and
yes, even the strap, if he didn't listen
and how happy he is about it
because look at how well he is doing.
Great job, *love it* (you can guess whose emphasis),
great pension, great kids.
But, let me tell you something,
discipline your kids.
My kids—they talk back, to their room.
I try not to hit them, but if I have to...
they really need it when they are teens.
(Crescendo emphasis)

> No princesses in my household
> and that includes the boys.
> If you want your kids to be really good, to live a healthy life,
> you've got to break the back of their willfulness.
> It's for their own good.

Q: I am sure there are many examples of the perniciousness of mechanical ethics.

Ba: Do any come to mind?

Q: How about the abstract virtue of "thou shalt not commit adultery"? If virtue means abstaining from sex with a married person, then over half the American population is not virtuous. But the notion of virtue remains a citadel of mechanical ethics and a tool for self-righteous people to try to control others.

Ba: Mechanical ethics attempt to be all-powerful. Punishment for violation follows into the hereafter, either dictated by reincarnation or judgment by an omniscient being. Typical methods of enforcement include invoking scripture, judging natural propensities as sinful (sex, use of intellect, questioning authority), and institutionalizing and decreeing the "correct" behavior in intimate relationships (marriage and parenting).

Q: You are describing the path of mechanical ethics. We seem to go from external voices that insist on acceptance of their agenda to internalizing those voices as if they are our own.

Ba: At that point, the voices and the ethics become introjected. That voice says: First, try as hard as you can, and then some. You can do better. There is always another goal to achieve and ever more room for perfection. Second, you are part of a team with a great tradition behind you, with a pantheon of heroes and martyrs to live up to and with a huge bevy of fans and loyalists urging you on. Last, don't disappoint or you could end up in hell, or come back as a slug or not be welcomed by your ancestors after you die. So do not be lazy. Do not be helpless. Strive to become; do not let anyone down. Follow secular and scriptural law and you will be good. You probably will be rewarded with prosperity in this life and most certainly with a better afterlife.

Q: You certainly will be ready to condition your own children. The machine runs smoothly onwards.

Ba: One question remains: Who is in control?

Ordinary Extraordinary Experiences

Ba: Everyone has ordinary extraordinary experiences that challenge mechanical ethics. Intimate sexual embrace, the unbridled care for a child, majestic feelings in nature, flashes of meaningful insight, the death of a loved one, and aesthetic expression, all undermine allegiance. The sheer horror of war, of prejudice, or of deliberate cruelty visited upon a friend or an ethnic group challenges mechanistic beliefs. Couples who feel romantic love will defy their families and their clan. Aesthetic impulses demand to be satisfied. The death of a loved one, especially when unexpected, can undermine religious and ritual practices. The horror of war forces us to question the wisdom of the clan and country.

Q: I have had many of these types of experiences. I am sure that others have had them as well. Why, then, do mechanical ethics persist?

Ba: Unfortunately, the value of ordinary extraordinary experiences usually lacks sufficient power to offset the daily conditioning that permeates home, school, politics, media, law enforcement, movies, athletics, economics, houses of religious worship, and most human thoughts. Liberating insights are ultimately rationalized by comments like "You were just under a lot of stress from the suddenness of the death" or "I had my fling and now it is time to get back to the real world" or "No one can expect this love to last forever." These self-imprisoning statements arise because once mechanistic ethics become introjected; they grind away below the surface, attacking every challenge continuously. The statements seem normal and when another mechanistic comment from a parent, priest, or president, (or boss, or TV program, or…) reminds us of the conventional path, it seems "right" to return to the fold.

Q: How sad!

Ba: Staggering, insidious social consequences ensue due to the neglect of the value of ordinary extraordinary experiences. Liberation from Me is undermined, and many feel no hope of escape. Their need to consume and abuse escalates. The number of addicts and culturally defined outcasts escalates. The number of politicians committed to ever more narrowing views of ethics escalates. The need to prove we are right escalates, and with it, the attendant wars and prejudice. Right and wrong narrow. To be wrong is to be bad; to be wrong is to fail; to be wrong is a disgrace and cause for humiliation.

Another stultifying consequence is devaluation of non-ordinary experience. This limits the social contribution of explorers who directly experience the non-ordinary realms. Consequently, these explorers cannot share the ethics of their experience. They do not get the necessary feedback and support to refine and express their ethics. Those who have travelled the non-ordinary realms then have difficulty finding the contextual frame in which their new insights can be expressed for the benefit of others.

Q: I agree and I think this so important. Most of us believe that non-ordinary experiences include the ability to bring forth realizations without further social support. But such expereinces do need that support and Me cannot provide it.

Ba: What is heartbreaking is that the richness of the human ethical capacity suffers. Tolerance, an inevitable result of integrated non-ordinary experiences, remains a concept for most. Tolerance thus loses the ethical validation and power that direct experience brings. The results are haphazard and incomplete manifestations of empathy. Conscience, reduced to deciding between good and bad, is not seen as the locus of the human capacity to feel all the subtleties and nuances of all the feelings of the moment.

However, if there wasn't the real thing, there would be no counterfeit. Ordinary extraordinary experiences consciously engaged and properly integrated dissolve mechanistic ethics. They replace Me with I.

Q: What are the ethics of I?

Here are poems describing I's ethics.

Indentured to Death

Religion is indentured to death
In every breath it takes.
Thereby suffering the bitter irony
Of negating eternal life
Now

Indenture costs.
Consider:
Priest abuse
A fundamentalist-driven Iraq war

(On all eight sides)
Largest land owner
Largest healthcare provider
Paying no taxes
Unwanted children
Support for Fascism
Ten percent of everything.
But most expensive—
at prices that make me blush—
is the real estate in heaven.

Knowing death as part of life
does not indenture,
But celebrates wholeness,
time freedom,
illusion, and the dissolution of illusion.

Renunciation

If your life is an offering
Then it's all surrender.
Death-Not Death.

I am a generous man
And help others in a natural, easy way.

Then I went to a Buddhist retreat.
Spurred by the exhortations of the Tibetan holy man

Everyone lined up to take the bodhisattva vow.

You know the one.
Though the many beings are numberless I vow to save them all
Though the dharma is unattainable I vow to attain it.
Though passions are endless I vow to end them.
And the granddaddy of them all:
I vow to attain Buddhahood.

Why do you need to vow to save others
When we are all shards of wholeness?
Why do we need to end passions
When they carry deep, meaningful lessons?
Why do we need to attain the dharma
When dharma is all there is?
Where isn't Buddha mind?

Please leave the unknown alone.
Naked participation freed from reincarnation and heaven
Encourages exploration.
Encourages reaching to the depths
For what can be known.

This is Being
Nothing essential is missing.
No Me remains.
And all is poetry.

Q: Many of the poems that you include in our dialogue could be substituted for these two.

Ba: True. The move from Me to I requires self-trust. Allegiance gone, we take responsibility for our choices. We question. We no longer depend on institutions of any kind to decide right and wrong for us.

Q: In other words, we access conscience.

Ba: Yes, but not full access.

Q: What happens?

Ba: Repressed stores of anger and grief release when we realize all the time we wasted in the Me identity. It takes time to digest those emotions. Until we do that, we don't have the self-trust to actualize the whole of conscience.

Q: I see that in the poems you mention death several times. Is this the same as the existential insight that we must confront the fundamental actuality of our death in order to have free choice?

Ba: It is. I acknowledges personal mortality without the support of mythical or unverifiable beliefs. That acknowledgement inevitably occurs with the death of allegiance.

Q: Are there other openings of similar magnitude?

Ba: I knows that self-knowledge is a possibility and can prepare the ground for self-knowledge to become wholly present.

Q: How?

Self-Knowledge

Ba: The ethics of self-knowledge necessarily includes the full breadth of conscience. Therefore, the ethics of self-knowledge arises "as part" of the creative flow of need. The ethics are not actually a part of the creative flow of need, any more than our heart is a part of our body. No heart, no body. It is ridiculous to talk of bodies without a heart. If there is a live body, there is a heart. If there is self-knowledge there is the creative flow of need. Conscience and compassion permeate ethics.

Q: I find the way you talk of time challenging. Simultaneous arising of conscience, the creative flow of need, self-knowledge, and compassion implies the absence of cause and effect. Are you saying that a person living self-knowledge is free of time constraints—that there is no concern for past or future?

Ba: Past and future exist but they do not constrain.

Q: The simultaneity of living in the creative flow and acting ethically seems foreign. Ethics have been the subject of great debate in every philosophy. Do we bypass the philosophical inquiry? Don't we have to intellectually digest ethics before we can know if we are acting ethically?

Ba: "I" can engage the philosophy. Living in the creative flow of need is living philosophy. By the way, the word *philosophy* comes from the Greek and means the wisdom of love. I believe it is legitimate to flip it. Then philosophy means the love of wisdom.

Q: Either way, sign me up.

Ba: You are already signed up. Philosophy comes with the human form. We express our philosophy in the way we make meaning.

Q: But in the creative flow of need, we don't have to think about meaning or about ethics?

Ba: All ethical models become irrelevant with self-knowledge. Self-knowledge has no contingencies; it is not dependent. A person living self-knowledge can create philosophical models, or use existing models, if necessary. However, as there is no dependency, there is no reliance on myth, history, philosophy, psychology, or cosmology.

Self-knowledge does not mean that we have gained or achieved a store of ethical data that is called upon to meet a given situation. Achieving and storing have nothing to do with self-knowledge. The perception/action that serves well-being and wholeness is always available. With compassion as the operating ethical mode, there is only participation in the creative flow of need.

Q: How far does it go? Could a person living self-knowledge steal? Lie? Physically hurt someone?

Ba: Self-knowledge uses all behaviors and affects without prejudice. Peacefulness and calmness have their place, as do anger, hurt, or disappointment. Like nature itself, which lives as the tarantula as well as the butterfly, a human in self-knowledge may be cantankerous or friendly. Each is equally useful and each is equally beautiful.

Q: You didn't answer the question. Is there a limit?

Ba: I can only invite you to find out for yourself.

Poems about ethics and self- knowledge:

Silence

Once you've heard silence
It never leaves.

Listening to resonating gongs,
Sitting quietly,
Gardening, reading, writing poetry
Lifestyles of addictions

The End of Pollution

Earth lives in my hara.
We dance to the beat of our thudding hearts,
A spinning soliton free in deep space.
Exquisitely sensitive to one another's pain,
Love pervades.
And Life springs forth through endless cycles of time.

Chapter Eight:
Living Self-Knowledge

Q: You have spoken of a person living self-knowledge many times. I have several questions about how such a life is lived.

Ba: Sure. Ask away.

Q: Does living self-knowledge mean that you teach others? Is that part of the calling?

Ba: A person living self-knowledge knows of serious dangers in attempting to teach about self-knowledge. Despite their wishes, most people do not learn well from didactic teaching. Teaching about self-knowledge does not often create the best ambiance for being self-knowledge.

Q: Why? I wish to know all about it.

Ba: There are many reasons for this. The hubris attached to "teaching about" sabotages the appropriate step from learning about something to actualizing it. The crippling belief is that we know something if we have learned about it. Learning about something is only the first step as our educational institutions would be wise to remember.

Second, many well-meaning people mired in separation and desperately yearning for something to believe in will make self-knowledge into a religion, which seems the inexorable push of the separated mind.

Third, the creative flow of need rarely calls for fame or popularity. However, fame and popularity have been used by wise people as political measures to bring attention to a civil liberty or to humanitarian rights. The creative flow of need is creative, not reactive. It is not based on appraisal, or evaluation, or currently popular social and political goals, and it has nothing to do with profit. Activities serve emergent well-being in ways evident to the wise person, if not to others.

Q: Next question: Does a person living self-knowledge have human faults? Are they detached or somehow above human concerns?

Ba: As we noted, no outsider can discern the meaning and value of the behaviors and actions of a person living self-knowledge. Human as human can be, a wise person can and does live the spectrum of all emotions and behaviors. Judging a wise person's action based on their behavior can only happen if the judge uses their own imposed and assumptive standards. The judgment relies on history, convention, or the judger's biographical experiences and beliefs. The judgment is rooted in the past or in current interpretations of the past or in extrinsically conditioned ethics. In short, such judgment must be fear-based, or at best compensatory, and so distant from need. It tells more of about the judger than about the person living self-knowledge. Speculation that evaluates the behaviors and actions of a wise person is almost always gossip. This includes both glorification and vilification.

Q: Well, if the person living self-knowledge doesn't necessarily teach and I can't assess by behavior, how would I know if the person were living self-knowledge?

Ba: An internal sensing connects a person living self-knowledge and someone who wishes to engage in a meaningful relationship with that person. However, each of us must be wary of our interpretation of this sensing. Too often the yearning separated self takes over and the groupie within dominates. This groupie, often anxious to be sated, expresses itself in direct proportion to the degree of separation. The formula is something like this: The more belief in separation, the more dramatic the yearning to believe in something that will end separation. Allegiance to the "path" will be mistaken for self-knowledge. Pretentious spiritual teachers will sanctimoniously rationalize this allegiance. The individual will buy into a belief such as reincarnation, or adherence to a restricted life now for the good life in heaven, or fail to question tradition, or believe that they have to "overcome" their "non-spiritual" tendencies.

Knowing this, the person living self-knowledge will often avoid places conducive to this conditioning—such as places of worship and "spiritual" gatherings. Self-observation and self-inquiry will allow an individual to go in the right direction—back to their motivation. Learning the why of what they do they will avoid the trap of their own conditioning.

Q: Finding a wise person seems subtle. We have to have developed our own inner sensing to do it.

Ba: Or the person may find you.

Q: How?

Ba: Wrong question.

Q: Well, what are the consequences of following a false teacher? Some say it can lead to better things because the effort towards self-knowledge has value.

Ba: The argument that going through false teachers and teachings will eventually lead to discerning the real may be accurate for a few, but most will spend their life in blind allegiance. It is pure speculation that wandering in unnecessary suffering will eventually lead to its dissolution.

Q: What about wounded healers? Their suffering often leads them to support others afflicted as they once were.

Ba: And if they never had unnecessary suffering to begin with? What would their lives have been then? How did their wounds occur? Is it not separation and its attendant loneliness, striving, and confusion? Is it not better to work there, then after the fact?

Q: Yes, but what about people who suffer as children, who learn separation there? Do you address that?

Ba: I do. It is my life's work; my vocation. Working with children and families is the absolutely best leverage point for ending the confusion about separation. In fact, by supporting optimal well-being in children the illusion of separation never occurs.

Q: That sounds fanciful.

Ba: I can only point to my work with children, families, and education for the past 30 years.

Q: At least wounded healers are using the suffering for the good of others.

Ba: Perhaps. You cannot evaluate a person by their behavior. You have to go deeper.

Q: How do false teachers get their followers?

Ba: Many religious teachers use the setting of worship combined with emotional excitement to incite emotive reactions. This setting enhances their charisma, improves attendance, and gives "faith" to the flock. The entire charade muddies the waters for those wishing to connect with a person living self-knowledge, though there are some wise people who can and do use spiritual settings when authentic need arises.

Here is a hint. Meeting a person living self-knowledge will include at least some element that disturbs, irritates, frustrates, or angers. It may come in the most mundane of circumstances or the most exalted. We can sense the connection through the medium of self-observation.

Q: You said that a wise person might initiate the relationship.

Ba: Yes, but do not expect a person living self-knowledge to know the totality of their effect upon you. Sure, there is an effect. Its meaning and purpose only comes to life in the relationship. A wise person stays in the needs of the relationship, unaffected by the consequences, alert to the emergence and responsive to it.

Often the consequences are surprising. Need becomes the medium in which a sparkling synergy emerges that deepens each participant's self-knowledge. Problems turn into opportunities; resistance to chaos and change evaporates. If resistance persists, we learn where we cling and what value inheres in the clinging.

Q: Can we be certain these results will happen?

Ba: Self-knowledge is the end of certainty. Self knowledge entails freedom, utter freedom from valuing the known more than the unknown. Uncertainty sharpens all the senses; it lends crystalline clarity to the meaning of relationships as they are, right now, with whomever and whatever we are in contact with.

Q: How can you be certain about the value of the end of certainty?

Ba: That's cunning but only shows a play on words. The end of certainly refers to the limitations of positivism—the belief that truth can only be known by measureable events. Positivism is not knowledge and certainly (pun intended) not self-knowledge.

What is the attraction to certainty? Self-inquiry yields very interesting answers.

Q: What happens when certainty ends?

Ba: The end of certainty brings the birth of authentic responsibility. A person living self-knowledge is fully engaged, responsive, and responsible yet never certain and thus breathing the keen edge of full participation.

Q: This demolishes predictability of outcomes.

Ba: Exactly. The hope for predictable outcomes denies our uniqueness, denies emergence. It pretends that events are linear—that cause follows effect. You might as well believe that Earth is flat and the center of the Universe.

Knowing uncertainty (which is not an oxymoron or even a paradox) is an aspect of self-knowledge that many can appreciate. False responsibility, especially sanctimonious and self-righteous behavior, has long been shattered. Assertions transform into the questions that resound throughout all consciousness: Who am I? And how do I know what I know? And do I have confidence in that mode of knowing? Knowing uncertainty distinguishes those who are authentically responsible from those who are not.

Q: What about death? Death is certain.

Ba: A person living self-knowledge does not speculate about death. Is there more than life? Is time a human invention and not a universal standard? Does all that is familiar disappear with death? These questions live as ongoing inquires. But that says nothing about death itself. Death may or may not be "the end."

Q: What about non-ordinary experiences? Many who have these experiences claim knowledge of life after death.

Ba: Juxtaposing extraordinary experiences onto death rings false. Preying upon people's ignorance of death rings false. No one has come back. No one could predict another's experience even if they had returned from death. Know yourself and death will be what it must be.

Q: But life after death is the centerpiece of religion.

Ba: They may be right; they may be wrong. But despite what many think, religion has little spiritual value or meaning for wise people. It does not tell about God; each person has an indwelling spirit inexorably drawing them towards what religions call God. It does not define God; God is indefinable. It does describe God's nature; spirit unfolds as each of us, as our nature, as an emergent whole. Description and definition depend upon our participation in self-knowledge. This simple fact is not open to interpretation or any sort of equivocation.

Q: Does actualizing self-knowledge draw a person to work with the less fortunate?

Ba: A person living self-knowledge works where she works well. Working with the indigent or underprivileged has no greater worth than working with the wealthy. Underdogs and overdogs are an illusion. Ignorance is ignorance. Pain is pain.

A subtle, continual, palpable vibration lives within the heart of a wise person. It is the vibration of universal suffering. Wise people do not attempt to manipulate this vibration no matter how profound the attendant feelings. Perceptible only to genuine conscience, attunement to this vibration sounds the notes of compassion. It comes with the creative flow of need.

Q: Is self-knowledge everyone's destiny? Will the draw to self-knowledge be actualized by all humans in the same way as having two eyes or standing upright?

Ba: Beyond doubt, wise people know that the draw to self-knowledge spirals through every relationship, every entity, every event, and every being. There are those who believe that actualization of self-knowledge is inevitable for humanity. Inevitable is a long time. For me, it is a fruitless speculation. Here we are. Here is the opportunity. What will you do?

Q: So speculation about the future gets in the way?

Ba: For many of us it does.
With the awakening of self-knowledge, the meaning, purpose, and value of existence is known. And it is sacred. We cannot say why it is sacred, but it is known to be. For this knowledge we live. From this knowledge we engage. As this knowledge we participate.

Q: And that participation means openness and questions, not speculation and certainty?

Ba: Self-knowledge brings freedom to doubt, to question, to not predict, to not project the past into the future. Self-knowledge brings liberation to allow emergence, to respect and enjoy knowledge as fluid and alive, and to avoid the trap of knowledge as a fixed entity.

Q: And this is true for each of us?

Ba: Yes, each of us has the capacity for exquisite attunement to life-as-it-is and there, right there, lives self-knowledge. When concepts of containment and control dissolve, then liberation is known to have nothing to do with answers, nothing to do with information, nothing to do with logic, nothing to do with talent or genius. Each of these may have its relative place, but none of them validate or contradict liberation.

Q: You insist on a distinction between knowledge and the contents of knowledge. Yet that is hard to do, especially in emotionally charged moments. Is it really possible?

Ba: A person living self-knowledge has no doubt that the gift is knowledge itself and not the contents of knowledge. For instance, even in extreme sadness and grief, there is no loss of connection, no belief in separation, no alienation. Even in extreme good fortune, there is no belief in specialness or supremacy. For instance, the death of a loved one or the most exalted extraordinary experience engenders deep humility and vivification of meaning. The wise person does not identify with the dominant emotion. All content is fully felt, fully acknowledged. There is no imposition of logic or reason; no rationalization or justification that mitigates the gestalt of one's momentary consciousness. And in that gestalt lives self-knowledge, lives the unadorned fact that there is this self that is intimate, aware, impartial, and free.

Chapter Eight: Living Self-Knowledge

Those living self-knowledge participate in life and know life as the matrix in which we come to know ourselves. They know, they know that they know, and they live in ever opening knowledge.

Chapter Nine: Love

Q: Don't we have to talk about love?

Ba: As I promised, love must be given special consideration. Self-knowledge offers a unique participation in love, as love. As this perspective may be somewhat jarring, I would like to offer it in detail and without interruption. Then we can dialogue afterwards.

Q: In other words, my current beliefs are going to be challenged again. Okay, go ahead.

Ba: It's more than that. In the throes of love there is passion for love to be understood, for the mythic conceptions to be undermined, for love's inherent freedom to at least be recognized and ultimately known.

Q: Then, go ahead. Absolutely, just go right ahead.

Ba: Love destroys.
No human can fathom love. It is always a complete surprise, a gift beyond all reckoning, a bestowal beyond anything we expect or deserve, and for which we have

more gratitude than the capacity to express it. Love leaves us in constant debt to life, for life has found love and love irrefutably allows entry into a realm that transcends life. Love kills our conceptions of ourselves and leaves us naked, foolish, and, unless there is surrender, tumbling in chaos and confusion. Our entire life is drawn to love, to serving it. Love is the meaning inside the meaning, the essence of the essence, the redeemer of all of life's suffering. Love gives meaning to justice, freedom, and virtue. Love provides the essence of the creative flow of need. Touching the hem of love's fabric can send us into dizzying dancing for centuries. No metaphor begins to approximate love's nature; only imposter poetry wastes effort by trying to describe it.

Love destroys.

All possessiveness dissolves, all objectification falls to the a priori insight that love has no boundaries. Love is not event-driven and it is utterly independent of all that it permeates. Love has no opposite. Hate, possessiveness, jealousy oppose themselves. Hate corrupts the hater's heart, the possessors only possess their own concepts and images, and the jealous find only their own insecurity at the bottom of their envy. Love has no opposite.

We cannot love someone else. Loving someone else places the love in the person. All we can say is that due to some mysterious affinity, love arises in certain moments, in certain relationships for each of us. To claim to love someone is to claim to control love.

Love has no history and no tomorrow. No one knows when and how love arises. It's madness to assert that we will love another in the next instant or the next morrow. Many people access respect, caring, devotion, and passion when love disappears. Learning keeps the relationship meaningful. Others cannot bear the disappearance of love and end the relationship. Living love repeatedly with any person is rare indeed.

We cannot anticipate the actions love will demand. Today's expression becomes tomorrow's habit and love does not live as habit. *Fresh, alive, responsive, alert, intimate, aware,* even *overwhelmed* come close to describing the consciousness love induces, yet cultivating any or all of these will not guarantee love's appearance. To act a certain way to seduce love only pushes it away. To demand love from another pretends that love is theirs to give (though other desirable affects certainly are); to demand that your actions should produce love is a fool's errand. Many relationships die because of the mistaken notion that the people stopped loving each other, that they had a choice to love and then refused it.

Love destroys.

Only being enters love. Therefore love is never subservient to reason. Reason can sometimes get some sense of love's effect when it is very quiet and respectful and does not impose concepts, rules, and regulations. Surrender means surrender.

The yearnings of the persona often contribute to stimulating receptivity to love, but love obliterates persona. Persona may sing love's praises, may be lit by the experience of love, may yearn with a zealot's ferocity, and may adopt all sorts of pious postures. Nonetheless, the persona simply does not enter the realm of love. Memory, which is persona's principal sustaining device, cannot begin to approximate love. Sometimes the persona's romantic attempts at love are touching; more often the persona's homage to tradition inhibits access to love.

Love destroys.

Love takes away the right to murder for murder ends the possibility of love in this life. Thus, murder is the only absolute crime. Nothing condones murder whether it is done by an individual or a government. No supposed gain for the murderer can equal the loss of the possibility of knowing love. There are times when it may be necessary to take another's life, but these times are rare indeed. Certainly material gain, foreign policy, and revenge fail as adequate motivations for murder. State executions attempt to justify murder by murdering the murderer. The state does not consider that they are murdering that person's chance to know love.

Murder kills the murdered and the murderer. Denying the possibility of love to another person blinds us to love's existence. That blindness stretches and stretches. Worse, rationalizing the attendant feelings to murder brings counterfeit notions of love. Rigid and controlling relationships to family, to religion, to nation, and to ourselves take over. We become the walking dead. Soldiers who have killed and then cannot return to a connected life believe they have lost the right to love.

Love destroys.

False spirituality demands that love be given first, prior to directly experiencing love. We should love the savior or the deity. If we give our heart, then the deity will return the love. Since the supplicant wishes so deeply for love and for spiritual connection, they conjure up their best notion of love. The supplicant may even conjure a response by the object of their love. But love can neither be conceived nor conjured, and the process leads to fabricated beliefs about love that gains mob approval through thought consensus. The draw to love has been diverted; separation rules.

Love destroys.

Love destroys death. Love comes from nowhere and goes nowhere. Love does not move and has no dependencies. Death's movement is from life. Death entails the cessation of perceived time/space. Death depends upon belief in the body. Love reveals an inconceivable limitless truth and so suggests that the unknown is not bad or scary, or to be avoided. Death then finds its place as the necessary agent of change. Death is part of the creative flow of need but still once removed for the essence, from the meaning inside the meaning. Death can no longer be seen as ultimate. Death gives meaning to life, but not to that which transcends life.

Q: Whew! Now I need you to cite specific examples of love as destroyer.

Ba: You are a parent…

Q: I knew it. I knew this is where you were going. Yes, the first contact with my child destroyed my previous way of organizing my world.

Ba: How many children do you have?

Q: Two, and yes, the second one was as powerful as the first. Okay, what do you mean that I cannot love another? I love my spouse and my children.

Ba: If you can control love, then I assume that you would love everyone.

Q: I don't, not in the same way.

Ba: What do you mean?

Q: I wish the best for them. I also feel strong affinity for many. But I wouldn't use the word *love* for them in the same way I use it for my family.

Ba: How about yourself? Do you love yourself?

Q: I never thought about it. I see what you mean, though. Love includes a feeling and a commitment and gratefulness, but I have not looked at the source of these feelings.

Ba: And when you do, I don't think that you will take credit.

Singular experiences of love happen to almost everyone yet few trace the experience to the source—to love itself. Environmentalists will often tell of a transcendent moment in nature, overwhelmed by beauty, touched by knowing beyond thought, wrapped in inspired feelings of belongingness and trust and then perhaps love just as it is—timeless, without arising or decaying. And then they will think: I had this moment of love. And that is wrong direction. They are attempting to possess the experience. They will only end up with the memory.

Q: What happens then?

Ba: Different outcomes for different people. Many will become active in social justice issues. Some will keep returning to nature as they believe nature to be the source of the experience. Others may become religious or take greater interest in spiritual paths.

Q: Surely these are fine outcomes. Is there a problem here?

Ba: Yes. Attention is spent of the outcome of love participation, rather than the source. Nature is not the source, nor is a romantic partner. Confusing the source of love to be dependent on where a person is or with whom is the classic mistake of mistaking finger pointing to the moon for the moon itself. I often think of it this way: social justice, communion with nature, romantic engagement is moving downstream propelled by the energizing aftershock of love.

Going with the flow seems self evident and logical; it suggests increased opportunity to experience love and improving the social world.

But it is the wrong direction. Rather than flowing out, turn inwards. While it may seem counterintuitive, we must go upstream.

Q: I imagine that upstream means some sort of self inquiry.

Ba: Yes. Love destroyed all concepts; transcendence reigned. What does that mean to me, to you, to each of us?

Q: I see that murder eliminates the possibility of the murdered one knowing love but what about those who commit heinous crimes such as raping and killing children? It seems that you are asserting that they still might know love and therefore be redeemed, or even contribute to well-being. I cannot agree.

Ba: Why not?

Q: The kind of sickness that must exist to commit such a crime does not seem curable.

Ba: Why did you switch from love to sickness? What do we know about love? Can we confidently assert that we know love so well that we are certain it cannot affect the cure?

Q: No, I guess we don't. In truth, it is my hatred of the crime, my care for the victim, my unwillingness for the perpetrator to have a single good moment in life, and my fear that such people are allowed to live in my society that forms my perspective.

Ba: Thank you. That is very clear and has purchase in all of us. But it has little to do with love. I certainly would constrain perpetrators. I just wouldn't murder them. Also, I would be extremely skeptical of any claim they made about love. But I wouldn't murder them.

Q: I see that. And I don't dispute your insight that murdering murders the murderer. But what about war? Surely you would agree that Nazi Germany had to be defeated.

Ba: Do the self inquiry. When you have deeply inquired you will find the warrior's answer for yourself. Those warriors who self inquire will know how their actions affect them.

Q: But what about for you?

Ba: I know, and with all humility, I am a warrior.
  Again, love destroys the murderer in each of us. No matter the intensity of the bitterness or the feeling of righteousness attendant to revenge, when we murder under those conditions we murder our ability to love.

Q: Let's talk about death. You're comments about love change your statement about death.

Ba: How?

Q: You stated that we can question death, but we cannot know what it is. But here you talked about death as the end of time and an agent of change. Love destroys death, you claimed. How can you know it is destroyed if you don't know what it is?

Ba: I described the attributes of death from the perspective of self-knowledge. Those attributes of time and change do not define death any more than the size of the font defines a book. When I tell my child that love is forever, I mean just that. How do I know? I don't mean that the momentary feeling will endure forever. Rather, I know love in that moment and that knowledge includes the transcendence of time.

Q: Then love is self-knowledge; self-knowledge is love.

Ba: Yes. Exactly. But we are not talking about a thing, or a concept. Objectify and confuse; participate and awaken.

Q: And therefore compassion and the creative flow of need are love, are self-knowledge.

Ba: May I leave you with a poem?

Q: Sure.

Chapter Nine: Love

This poem sketches embrace in the midst of love:

Beyond

Gazing into my lover's eyes
In the midst of sexual embrace
Generations unfold.
There is my death, and hers.
Over and over and over,
Through countless life forms.

Presure grows from inside my chest,
Swelling with suffering.
Intense—something bursting
I can't hold on…

A rapier slices through my skin, through my ribs.
My vision is filled with my lover's eyes.
My senses solely focused on the soft pulsations
Of the deepest interior of her vulva.
While the suffering of humanity floods through.

I would cry out but there is no voice,
I would move to orgasm but there is no desire,
I would stop the bleeding but there is no resistance.

And in that timeless moment
Devotion breathes